THE SALVAGE CHEF
COOKBOOK

THE SALVAGE CHEF COOKBOOK

More Than 125 Recipes, Tips, and Secrets to Transform What You Have in Your Kitchen into Delicious Dishes for the Ones You Love

Michael Love
Specialty Chef at the World-Famous Epicure Gourmet Market & Café

Foreword by Robert Irvine
Photos by Lynn Parks

Skyhorse Publishing

Skyhorse Publishing books may be purchased in bulk at special discounts for sales promotion, corporate gifts, fund-raising, or educational purposes. Special editions can also be created to specifications. For details, contact the Special Sales Department, Skyhorse Publishing, 307 West 36th Street, 11th Floor, New York, NY 10018 or info@skyhorsepublishing.com.

Skyhorse® and Skyhorse Publishing® are registered trademarks of Skyhorse Publishing, Inc.®, a Delaware corporation.

Visit our website at www.skyhorsepublishing.com.

10 9 8 7 6 5 4 3 2 1

Library of Congress Cataloging-in-Publication Data

Love, Michael, 1962- author.
   The salvage chef cookbook : more than 125 recipes, tips, and secrets to transform what you have in your kitchen into delicious dishes for the ones you love / Michael Love, specialty chef at Epicure Gourmet Market & Cafe ; foreword by Robert Irvine ; photos by Lynn Parks.
      pages cm
   ISBN 978-1-62914-581-5 (hardback) -- ISBN 978-1-63220-113-3 (ebook) 1. Cooking. 2. Cooking (Leftovers) 3. Consumer education. I. Title.
   TX714.L675 2014
   641.5--dc23
                        2014033636

Cover design by Owen Corrigan
Cover photo credit Lynn Parks
Interior design by Sam Schechter

Print ISBN: 978-1-62914-581-5
Ebook ISBN: 978-1-63220-113-3

Printed in China

TABLE OF CONTENTS

FOREWORD

Over the past few decades, South Florida cuisine has evolved from providing uninteresting tourist food to an international culinary mix that rivals some of the great American cities. Miami, in particular, has benefited from not only strong Latin and Caribbean influences, but also cuisines and techniques from Asia, Europe, and the Mediterranean. Additionally, South Florida cuisine, its restaurants, and its markets benefit greatly from the wealth of fresh seafood, tropical fruits, and locally grown vegetables available year round. Though once a city known for its Art Deco hotels and weekend-long spring break parties, Miami now offers travelers and locals a plethora of trendy high-end contemporary American eateries and an ever expanding array of fusion cooking.

One constant in this growing and sophisticated culinary landscape has been Epicure Gourmet Market and Café, which was founded in the 1940s. As I hosted Epicure's Party: Impossible for the 2012 South Beach Wine & Food Festival, I got to know Epicure's owner, Jason Starkman, and their talented Specialty Chef Michael Love both personally and as colleagues. As we served and entertained more than 1,600 guests, I discovered their mutual innate enthusiasm about food. Additionally, I was so impressed when I sampled Michael's offerings that are part of the Epicure with Love line, and what struck me was not only Michael's creative all-natural approach to cooking, but his passion for sharing his knowledge with home cooks.

As the former host of programs with the titles *Dinner: Impossible* and *Worst Cooks in America* and current host of *Restaurant: Impossible,* I can assure you that, regardless of the popularity of cooking shows today, millions of cooks really don't know what to do with the food they currently have stored in their pantries and refrigerators and will benefit greatly from the *salvage* cooking skills, techniques, and recipes that Michael has detailed in this book.

Like many professional chefs, I can "taste" a dish just by reading the recipe, and I can promise you that you've got some delicious meals in store when cooking the dishes in this book. Michael is one of the upcoming stars in the constellation of the Miami food scene. His *Salvage Chef Cookbook* is a wonderful collection of dishes for cooks of all levels looking for ways to cut down on food waste, lower their food costs, and put contemporary spins on classic dishes.

—Robert Irvine

PREFACE

"Great food is like great sex. The more you have the more you want."
—Gael Greene

FOOD. We live it, we crave it, we savor it, we cook it, we watch it, and we even dream about it. Throughout the centuries, the kitchen has been the epicenter of family life. Today, it still is the place where we gather to plan our vacations and family gatherings, discuss sports, work schedules, have family powwows, do homework, invite a friend for coffee . . . It is a place where we make our shopping lists and think and talk food.

When I was about six years old, living in the suburbs of Long Island, New York, I spent many hours imagining myself as the star in the kitchen, creating marvelous dishes for my family to great applause. I often stayed home from school as I suffered from childhood asthma. My mother would make me tea with milk and honey and white toast with butter and jelly. As I devoured this simple yet delicious breakfast, I would avidly watch TV shows all morning and into the afternoon. In the late 1960s and early '70s, there were only two cooking shows on television, Julia Child's *The French Chef* and Graham Kerr's *The Galloping Gourmet*. Graham Kerr was fascinating to watch. He would run through the audience with a forkful of chicken covered in some butter-laden sauce and lovingly feed it to an adoring Graham fan who would proceed to roll her eyes back and moan in a food orgasm as the camera panned across his captivated followers. *I could do that. If I could just talk with that accent, tie a silk scarf around my neck, and wear tight pants, I could do that.*

I had already developed an interest in cooking from my mother, her mother, and most of all, Louise, our wonderful cook from Savannah, Georgia, who worked first for my great-aunt, then for my grandmother (who stole her from my great-aunt), and eventually for my mother. Early on, my grandmother taught Louise to cook many of the traditional Jewish dishes our family loved like brisket, roast chicken with dark gravy, chopped liver, and matzo-ball soup. She took those recipes and added her own special touches, creating the richest brown gravy ever, the deepest deep-dish apple pie with a layer of crust in the middle, the spiciest pumpkin pie served with thick whipped cream, and the darkest, richest chocolate cake with amazing buttercream frosting.

Louise reciprocated by teaching my grandmother how to make the crispiest, crunchiest southern fried chicken. Between the scents in the kitchen, which would draw me in like a cartoon character floating horizontally on a visible aroma trail, and watching my two favorite cooking shows, I discovered not only a love for the kitchen, but also an affinity for food and a talent for cooking.

From the two shows on TV back in the '60s to more than two hundred shows per week on a dozen or more channels mainly dedicated to cooking, the world is waking up to not only a diverse spectrum of cuisine, but also cooking techniques, celebrity chefs, spices, competitions and cook-offs, butter, bacon, throwdowns, and a *culinary point of view.* Top chefs, caterers, grandmothers, short order cooks, and home cooks all know fundamental formulas for cooking good food: fresh ingredients, simple layers of flavor, and a solid, proven technique. However, many of these same people, professional and home cooks, are often at a loss when it comes to using their considerable culinary skills on previously purchased food that is left languishing in the fridge, breadbox, or pantry. Perfectly good food is too often thrown out because it is a few days from peak freshness or has passed its expiration date.

While working as the specialty chef at Epicure Gourmet Market in Miami Beach, I spent a good amount of time in the meat department and created many cooked food items from the fresh meat, poultry, and seafood that came in daily. One day, I discovered that approximately forty pounds of chicken trim was being thrown away each week. The "trim" is the tenderloin (commonly known as "chicken tenders") and fat trimmings discarded when fabricating a chicken cutlet. Although Rudi (Epicure's butcher extraordinaire) made every attempt to use the trim for chicken sausage or chicken patties, there was just too much of it. When he asked me if I could do something with the trimmings, I suggested a chicken meat loaf that would incorporate roasted vegetables, fresh herbs, and a savory glaze made from harissa, red pepper tapenade, and ketchup. The next day we went to work on the recipe, created four large loaves of chicken meat loaf, and placed it on the hot foods line at Epicure. It sold out in less than an hour and so was born my new unofficial title, The Salvage Chef.

Although food is my passion, I actually began the professional phase of my life as a musician. But the transition from piano to pots and pans was actually completed almost twenty years ago, and now many more have seen me demonstrate how to "make three soups in less than an hour" or "the perfect weekend brunch" than have heard me play after attending Berklee College of Music in Boston.

As an apprentice, I entered the professional kitchen, first at Cappy's in the Back Bay area of Boston, tossing pizzas and learning to become a grill cook, and then at the highly acclaimed Versailles Restaurant in suburban Arlington, Massachusetts, where I witnessed French cooking at the highest level from famed chef Isaac Dray.

I moved to Florida in 1996 and a year later became the founding chef at Tabu Grill & Bar, a popular late night spot in Sunny Isles Beach known for its Mediterranean flavors.

Leaving the professional kitchen for a time, I amassed a loyal following as a private chef and cooking instructor. In addition to offering classes at such noted spots as Bloomingdales and Williams-Sonoma stores, I created a cooking class series called *Cooking with Love*, which was featured on *Deco Drive*, a popular nightly entertainment TV show in South Florida.

As a cooking class instructor, I first encountered Jason Starkman, whose family owns Epicure Gourmet Market & Café in South Florida, as well as the chain of Jerry's Famous Deli restaurants in California and Florida. Epicure hosted the *Cooking with Love* series in 2010 that earned me the moniker of "culinary guru" from the *Miami Herald* (March 14, 2010).

The following year, Jason hired me as Epicure's specialty chef with the purpose of creating and launching a new line of co-branded all-natural gourmet food products called Epicure with Love, or as Jason calls it: "five-star in a jar." The continuously expanding line of all-natural food, which launched in November 2011, now includes ten different soups, prepared foods, entrées, and desserts.

In addition to product development for the Epicure with Love line, I am also the off-premise chef for Epicure's high-end catering events and continue to use my "salvage" skills and innovations to create delicious prepared foods for Epicure's stores.

My inspiration for writing this cookbook was Michele. When we first starting dating around four years ago, she would ask me what I liked to do in my spare time. I told her I loved to cook. She immediately responded with "Women *love* men who can cook!" After several romantic dinners, I told her I was thinking of writing a cookbook for men. She encouraged me and supported me throughout the recipe development stages and finally pushed me to begin a manuscript, which, after three years, transformed into *The Salvage Chef Cookbook*. She continuously gives me innovative ideas for recipes and comes up with unique flavor combinations that I incorporate into my cooking.

INTRODUCTION

Every day families throw away perfectly edible yet overlooked food as they are often unaware of how to "salvage" it and create something delicious. I was shocked to find out that, by far, the number-one category of waste in the United States is food leftovers and food preparation scraps (trim) from restaurants, cafeterias, and households. Moreover, food waste in America has increased more than 50 percent over the last forty years, totaling more than thirty-three million tons each year. On average, supermarkets across the country discard 12 to 14 percent of the produce they buy, simply for aesthetic reasons. It is clear there is a huge economic and environmental impact from this waste, and it can't help but shift our thinking on how we treat food, from purchase to preparation to plate.

Many restaurants across the country are participating in the popular "farm to table" movement by patronizing local farms for their produce and meats. While this is a worthwhile endeavor, what is lost on most Americans is the amount of food thrown out. Even worse, while we continue to buy in bulk, throw away expired food, and scrape literally tons of food into the garbage every day, more than seventeen million American households are considered "food insecure," meaning they are finding it difficult to feed everyone in the family.

Currently, food waste in America is up 16 percent from last year alone, while nearly fifty million people are on food stamps.

Coming to the rescue is the *Salvage Chef Cookbook*. As the specialty chef at Epicure Gourmet Market & Café in Miami Beach, I've built a reputation as the Salvage Chef by finding creative ways to transform food trimmings, excess food product, and items that may not be saleable in their present condition, into delicious gourmet food.

As a chef and cooking teacher in Florida, I've developed a large following for my cooking classes and demonstrations because of my emphasis on fun and useful cooking tips, essential techniques, and my passion to show home cooks how to become salvage chefs in their own kitchens.

Salvage to most people means saving something that has been discarded. To me, salvaging in the kitchen is about taking real food destined for the trash bin and finding an innovative and delicious purpose for it, thereby saving money, reducing waste, and delivering delicious food to the table. *How about "farm to table to tummy"?*

My style of cooking is to create new twists to old favorites so food is simultaneously familiar, fresh, and exciting. The *Salvage Chef Cookbook* includes more than one hundred scrumptious recipes, some of which come from my co-branded line of products, Epicure with Love, carried at the Epicure markets.

The beginning chapters focus on must-have "salvage" appliances, proper food storage, how to cut down on food waste, creatively working with leftovers, and suggested expiration periods for most raw and cooked food items.

The first collection of recipes includes my spice blends ("Love Rubs"), basic sauces and marinades, and answers to the ever-nagging culinary dilemma: "To salvage, or not to salvage? That is the question." Some food items are on the edge of freshness or just sitting around the kitchen and have their place in a delicious marinade, while other food items can be revived or used in support of a fresh ingredient. Every recipe highlights the "salvage" or leftover items in the ingredients list, but all can be prepared with fresh ingredients. This makes the *Salvage Chef Cookbook* a complete and comprehensive cookbook for households looking to stretch their food dollars, home cooks who want to make better use of their leftovers, and experienced cooks who will just *love* the delicious recipes.

Another innovative section of the book is the Salvage Index, which provides the reader with an extensive list of leftover and *salvageable* items used in *The Salvage Chef Cookbook* recipes.

My hope is that after cooking a few of my recipes, you will get creative with your ingredients and create your own "salvage" versions of my dishes. Salvage it, savor it, and *love* it!

CHEF'S NOTES:

- All olive oil is extra-virgin olive oil.
- All butter is unsalted.
- All flour is all-purpose unless specified.
- All black pepper is freshly ground black pepper.
- All salt is coarse kosher salt.
- Unless otherwise specified, use large eggs.
- Oven temperatures are based on using conventional ovens, not air assisted or convection.

CHAPTER 1: TOOLS OF THE TRADE

"A jazz musician can improvise based on his knowledge of music. He understands how things go together. For a chef, once you have that basis, that's when cuisine is truly exciting."

—Charlie Trotter

First off, let's take stock of *your* current kitchen inventory. You may have a well-equipped kitchen and a fully stocked pantry. *Should that be the case, then this section doesn't apply to you.* However, if it's like many household kitchens across America, it most likely includes a mismatched collection of silverware, a variety of colored cereal bowls, and three beer mugs. *I'll bet you five dollars that one of those mugs is engraved with your alma mater or someone's favorite sports team.* Let's continue: one airport shot glass, a set of fancy china you refuse to use, bottle opener, warped cutting board, impossible-to-open-the-wine wine opener, a large all-purpose knife that can barely cut through softened butter, two steak knives, a can opener that gets about two-thirds of the way around the can and leaves a trail of barbed wire, an extra-large non-stick frying pan with most of the Teflon scratched off, and five basic dinner plates. *Still can't figure out where that sixth plate is?* We will round off this classic culinary collection with a small pot for boiling water that is too small for pasta so I don't know what you would use it for, other than boiling water for tea. And let's not forget the large barbeque utensils for the gas grill. *Another five says you don't own a gas grill.*

As far as plug-in items, you probably have a toaster oven (circa 1980-something), a microwave oven, a "Bullet" that is missing many parts, a blender that you haven't used since that New Year's Eve party when you made one too many frozen margaritas, and who can forget the old crock pot that was handed down from your mother-in-law. Sound familiar?

I may be exaggerating just a bit, but you get the point. Technique is everything. Having the right equipment to facilitate that technique is key. You don't need to invest in an $800 mixer or a $400 Le Creuset enameled pot, but you *will* need the basics to be effective and proficient in the kitchen. What follows are the utensils and equipment that will make your *salvage* storing, prepping, and cooking more efficient.

Airtight Storage Containers

For ease and efficiency in storing dry goods, leftovers, and unused portions of lemons, onions, vegetables, stock, etc., have on hand several sizes and shapes of containers. They should be airtight and usable for the freezer.

Cookware

This could be the most important category of "equipment" for your kitchen. Using inferior cookware means poor and uneven heat transference, which leads to burning and sticking, which in turn leads to ruined food. A basic rule is "the heavier the better." There are stainless steel pots and pans, cast iron, copper plated, non-stick, and a plethora of options. Calphalon® and All-Clad® are the two most popular brands, but many celebrity chefs have inexpensive, decent quality cookware that can be easily found in most of the stores previously mentioned as well as from online retailers. You get the best value when you purchase your initial cookware in a "set." Keep it simple and don't spend a fortune. If you are a novice and don't want to take the time to *season* your pans after each use, choose non-stick for the first three pans listed below. Initially, I would recommend stainless steel for all your pots.

Here is your cookware shopping list:

- One large 16-inch skillet—the bigger the better. Look for one with steep sides of 2 inches or more
- One smaller 8-inch frying pan (for cooking eggs, sautéing a small amount of vegetables, or pan frying chicken, meat, or fish)
- One 12-inch frying pan with oven-friendly handle
- One large pasta pot with pasta strainer (usually comes as a set)
- One 8-quart heavy-bottomed large stock pot or soup pot
- One medium pot (also known as a Dutch oven, 5 to 6 quarts)
- One cast iron skillet (at least 12 inches)

Cutting Boards

A well-stocked kitchen can never have enough cutting boards. I recommend an all-purpose wood "butcher block"–type cutting board, preferably a thick, large, acacia wood or rock maple board. It could cost around $80 but, if you take good care of it, it will last for many years. Also, purchase one or two plastic or polyethylene cutting boards for cutting proteins, one of which should be just about as large as the wooden block and the other one a bit smaller.

Tip: To avoid cross contamination when working with raw proteins (chicken, fish, pork), you will want to use a plastic cutting board and make sure no other foods are cut simultaneously on that board.

You may want to designate your plastic cutting boards for just proteins. To keep the plastic board from sliding all over your countertop, slightly dampen two folded paper towels and place them on your wooden butcher block. Then place the plastic cutting board on top of the wet paper towels. The plastic board will now stay in place.

Grater

Most well-stocked kitchens have what is known as a box grater. It's hollow, open at one end, and has four different grating options. If you don't have a food processor yet (which you will soon), much of the fine slicing and shredding you might need to do with vegetables can be accomplished using the box grater. I suggest you also have a minimum of two graters besides the box grater: an all-purpose, one-sided grater primarily for cheese and a smaller grater for finer grating that will also work well as a zester. Down the road, you might want to get a bit fancy and invest in a microplane (for zesting) and a mandolin, which is an appliance that slices and dices with great ease and consistency.

Grill Top/Griddle (or Grill Pan)

Grill tops and grill pans are great for grilling chicken and other meats because you get a good sear on the flesh and the fat drips into the crevices, giving you a healthier option. Griddles are key for pancakes *(Vanilla Pancakes, page 84)*, French Toast *(Challah French Toast with Crispy Ham and Roasted Apples, page 67),* and a variety of searing where you need maximum surface area contact. The best option here is the grill top/griddle combo. It's a raised grill top on one side and a flat griddle on the other and is long enough to cover two burners. There are non-stick versions, but I have always had great success with the heavy cast-iron variety.

Grinder

This appliance can become one of your best friends for *salvaging* food in your kitchen. The easiest approach here is to purchase a grinder attachment to your stand mixer. If you don't have a stand mixer, there are stand-alone grinders you can use for ground beef, sausage making, and my favorite, chicken trim!

Immersion Blender

This is a wand-shaped appliance that has rotating blades at one end, which are housed in a round plastic compartment for safety. This hand-held blender is typically "immersed" into a soup pot or turkey roasting pan (after taking the turkey out) to quickly purée its contents without having to remove to a blender or food processor.

Kitchen Towels

You can never have enough small kitchen towels. I would suggest you reserve one or two of them for contact with food (*Crispy Potato and Turkey Sausage Hash Browns, page 81*) and wiping off excess sauces or drips from your serving plates. The other towels can be used for cleaning.

Mason Storage Jars

These are great for dry ingredients such as flour, sugar, pastas, etc. They are airtight and keep out moisture. You can also store sauces, dressings, and leftovers in your mason jars and they will do well in the refrigerator. *Michele and I love to drink iced tea and our favorite cocktails out of mason jars.*

Meat Hammer

A meat hammer is primarily used to tenderize cutlets of meat or poultry. A two-sided hammer is recommended since certain proteins such as flank steak sometimes require the "raised" side of the hammer, while chicken and veal are usually pounded thin with the flat side.

Meat Thermometer

You can check the cooking temperature of meat and poultry many ways without a thermometer, but I would recommend that you have one as a reliable indicator. Most meat can be timed for temperature and you can become proficient in "feeling" the temperature by pressing down on the meat with your finger; however, poultry is a bit more difficult to predict. Inserting a meat thermometer into the thickest part of a turkey or chicken is the best way to ensure your bird is fully cooked. Most meat thermometers are less than $15 and come with proper cooking temperatures for meat, chicken, etc.

Mini Food Processor

Ah, my favorite appliance. They are less than $30, have dozens of uses, and are fairly easy to clean. Most have grinding and chopping blades, as well as slicing blades that fit on the top to slice cheese, onion, potatoes, cabbage, and more. Since many of my dishes use a mini food processor to purée small vegetable pieces, it is important that you purchase an appliance whose main purée blade sits close to the bottom of the plastic container. You don't want the blades to pass over the smaller pieces. When you are able to, purchase a full-size food processor that can handle more volume and a variety of mixing jobs unsuitable for your mini.

Ramekins

I prefer two sizes of ramekins and a quantity of six each. A 4-ounce ramekin is perfect for sampling. It can be used for olives, raisins, nuts, compound butter, dipping sauces, and many other uses involving condiments. I also use it for egg dishes such as *Bacon, Onion, and Olive Souffliche* (page 74). The 8-ounce ramekin can be used for all of the above as well as for individual *Bacon, Truffle 4-Cheese Mac 'N' Cheese* (page 222), and other single-portion dishes.

Wraps

You will find uses for all three, so make sure you have plastic wrap, foil, and parchment paper (or wax paper).

> Note: It's worth mentioning that none of the above wraps should be used in the microwave. Plastic and wax can melt and no metal substance should go into a microwave oven. Remove all your food and ingredients from the wrap and place on a microwavable plate or bowl.

Zester

Also known as a microplane, this mini-grater effectively removes the peel from citrus fruits; the peel is where all the oils reside. It can also be used to create chocolate shavings or grind fresh nutmeg.

CHAPTER 2: STOCK UP ON THE BASICS

"Tomatoes and oregano make it Italian; wine and tarragon make it French. Sour cream makes it Russian; lemon and cinnamon make it Greek. Soy sauce makes it Chinese; garlic makes it good."

—Alice May Brock

There is nothing more frustrating than craving some delicious homemade soup, making your grocery list, buying all the fresh vegetables, and midway through the cooking process realizing that you don't have any bay leaves. Or thinking you have everything you need for Caesar dressing only to find a dried up lemon-half in the back of the refrigerator that, when squeezed, seemed to actually moan as it let out two drops of juice.

Being a salvage chef in your own kitchen can be a transformational experience, especially when you put together a delicious dish or meal with the food you already have on hand. However, having a well-stocked pantry, as well as frequently used staples, is most helpful. What follows is a list of pantry items (non-refrigerated) that should always be available for use in your kitchen.

Baking Powder

Made of mostly sodium bicarbonate (baking soda) and about one-third cream of tartar, baking powder is used to add volume and lighten the texture of cakes, muffins, and other baked goods. Baking powder causes an acid-based reaction that releases carbon dioxide into the batter or dough. As a general rule of thumb, 1 teaspoon of baking powder is usually the correct amount to rise 1 cup of flour with 1 cup of liquid and 1 egg.

Baking Soda

Baking soda lacks the acidity of baking powder and can be substituted for baking powder in recipes that have an acidic ingredient such as chocolate, yogurt, or buttermilk. (If you used baking powder with those acidic ingredients, the acid in the baking powder wouldn't be utilized in the reaction and might end up causing a bitter taste.)

Cocoa Powder (unsweetened)

Natural cocoa powder is dark, bitter, and imparts a deep chocolate flavor. Don't confuse this unsweetened cocoa powder for the *sweetened* cocoa drink mixes. They are not the same and are *not* interchangeable. *My favorite is Scharffen Berger, but Ghirardelli and Hershey are popular brands that may be more accessible from your local grocer.*

Cornmeal

I prefer stone ground and find it a bit more flavorful than fine ground. This is because some of the husk and germ is retained. Blue cornmeal is very popular as well and comes from the rarer blue corn variety.

Dry Mustard

Also known as ground mustard or powdered mustard, this is simply ground mustard seeds. Great for cheese spreads, sauces, dressings, and many cold salads such as potato, egg, and macaroni. My favorite uses include salad dressings, my *BBQ Spice Blend* (page 34), as well as a great dry rub on chicken or meat. The most popular is the almost two hundred-year-old brand Colman's® in a 2- or 4-ounce yellow canister.

Flour

All-purpose flour can be used for any baking recipe that requires flour. For breads, you may want to look for bread flour that has higher gluten content. Although it is not a pure white color, unbleached is preferred as it does not go through the chemical bleaching process.

Honey

There are many varieties of honey; however, Golden Blossom is a mild all-purpose variety and will work in just about every situation that requires honey.

Kosher Salt

Unlike common table salt, Kosher salt doesn't contain iodide or any other additives and has larger salt grains. This makes is easier to work with and control the amount of seasoning. In all of my recipes that list salt, I suggest Kosher salt; however, I do prefer fine grain salt for baking.

Oils

Every kitchen should have a good quality extra-virgin olive oil, a bottle of canola oil, or vegetable oil for frying. The olive oil is for finishing dishes, salad dressings, sauces, and can be used to sauté in situations where flavor is needed and the temperature is medium to medium-high. Canola has a higher burn point so you can sear meat, chicken, pork, and fish at a higher temperature without burning the oil, as you could easily do with olive oil. Additionally, canola oil doesn't impart any noticeable flavor.

Sugar

Your pantry should have white granular sugar, brown sugar (light or dark), and powdered sugar, referred to as confectioners' sugar in recipes that follow. I would also suggest a small container of superfine sugar, which dissolves better in cold drinks such as sangria, lemonade, iced tea, etc.

Tomato Paste

Usually available in a small 4-ounce can or 2-ounce tube, tomato paste is simply tomato solids (not including skins or seeds) and is used to enrich sauces and stews. It's always a good idea to have some on hand.

Vanilla Extract

Pure vanilla extract is what you are looking for here. The "pure" designation ensures a higher concentration of natural vanilla bean as opposed to imitation vanilla, which is chemically processed vanillin.

Vinegar

There are dozens of vinegars ranging from malt vinegar to wine vinegars, fruit based, rice, and more. This sounds like overkill but I assure you it is not. Stock your pantry with three vinegars:

1) white distilled vinegar, which is perfect as a common cleaning agent for coffee makers and can also be used when poaching eggs;
2) balsamic vinegar, which is great for sauces, dressings, or simply added along with extra-virgin olive oil on a salad; and
3) white wine vinegar, which is a great all-purpose variety for dressings. You can always experiment with different vinegars for variety.

Whole Tomatoes

Canned whole tomatoes are an invaluable staple in your pantry. They can be used in a wide variety of dishes, such as soups, stocks, sauces, and chili. They impart a deep rich tomato flavor and are far easier to use than fresh ones. San Marzano tomatoes, which are a variety of the plum tomato, are considered by most chefs as the best "sauce" tomato. Typically, they come in 14- or 28-ounce cans. Always have a couple of cans in your pantry.

CHAPTER 3: DON'T THROW IT AWAY

"You don't have to cook fancy or complicated masterpieces—just good food from fresh ingredients."

—Julia Child

What my childhood heroine Julia Child didn't mention when she said the above quote is how much food most households throw away due to excess or bulk purchasing and expired dates of food items. Much of the waste can be avoided with proper food storage practices and some creative *salvage* techniques and recipes. This chapter includes ideas for storing pantry items, increasing their shelf life, and instructions on properly handling and storing meat, poultry, and fish. I will also cover how to keep breads fresher for a longer time and how to transform day-old bread. Other *salvage* techniques and tips include what foods can be refrozen after thawing and how to tell if eggs are still fresh enough to use.

Many people simply don't know when a certain food has gone bad, or what food items need to be refrigerated after opening to stay fresh. Additionally, knowing the approximate expiration time frames of pantry and refrigerated items could save households thousands of dollars per year in wasted food.

BREAD

Aside from plate scrapings at the end of each meal, no other food item gets tossed in the trash more often than bread. Obviously, if bread is moldy, its long journey from raw ingredients to kneading, rising, chemistry, the perfect temperature and bake time, cooling, slicing, packaging, travel time, and store merchandising has come to a regrettable end—the trash bin. However, just because your bread may no longer be worthy of the sandwich board, it may still have many delicious destinies beyond its freshness threshold. What follows is not only the proper storage techniques for breads of all types to make them last longer, but some of the life-extending revivals and transformations that will not only save money but will liven up many dishes and meals when in combination with just-bought or on-hand ingredients.

Storage

Breads should be stored in a cool, dry place away from direct sunlight, such as a cabinet or deep kitchen drawer (around 68°F), not in the refrigerator. *I know you've been told it lasts longer in the fridge, but the taste will suffer.* The starch molecules dry out six times faster in the refrigerator ("retrogradation") and this causes the bread to lose moisture. One example is commercial, packaged breads that contain preservatives to slow down the retrogradation process.

Breads from the bakery should be left in their original wrapper to keep the exteriors crispy. Only slice what you intend to consume, as these fresh no-preservative artisanal breads will dry out within hours.

My suggestion on all bread, except baguettes (which are really designed as a daily bread), is to freeze half of what you buy. Use an airtight freezer bag and remove all the air before placing in the freezer. When you take the bread out of the freezer, make sure you thaw it in the freezer bag at room temperature so it can remoisturize itself. Popping just-thawed bread or refrigerated slices in the oven for 2 to 3 minutes at 350°F will crisp up the crust. Keep in mind the bread will go completely stale within a few hours so it will need to be consumed right away.

Additional Tips on Keeping Bread Longer

- When reaching into a plastic bag of bread, only touch the slices you will be taking out to eat. By touching the other slices in the bag you will be transferring bacteria inadvertently from your fingers to the bread, which will grow rapidly and cause the bread to get moldy much faster.

- If storing artisanal or home-baked bread in the freezer, it is best to slice it right before you place it in the storage bag. Frozen or thawing bread is difficult to cut and you may only want to use a few slices at a time.

Breadcrumbs

Breadcrumbs are the simplest of bread transformations; however, their many uses can be overlooked and underappreciated. You can easily prepare two types of made-from-day-old-bread breadcrumbs. Fresh breadcrumbs are best for breading on croquettes, fish, and chicken. Toasted breadcrumbs make delicious toppings for casseroles, pastas, and vegetable dishes.

To make fresh breadcrumbs, cut the crusts off the slices of bread and cut into 1-inch cubes. Pulse in a food processor until you have crumbs. If you want to season them, this is a good time to do it. I would suggest taking out half the breadcrumbs and storing them in an airtight container *without* any seasoning. Season the remaining breadcrumbs in the food processor by adding a pinch of salt, your favorite dried or fresh herbs, cayenne pepper (for spicy crumbs), and no more than a ½ teaspoon of extra-virgin olive oil to adhere the herbs and salt to the breadcrumbs. You can also make sweet breadcrumbs to sprinkle on desserts by adding equal amounts of sugar and cinnamon (about ½ teaspoon each). *It's great to have a few different types of fresh breadcrumbs on hand with different flavors. No reason to buy breadcrumbs.*

For toasted breadcrumbs, take the crustless bread cubes and place on a baking sheet and set in a 200°F oven until dry and crisp (for about 10 to 15 minutes) but not browned. Let cool for 5 minutes and pulse in the food processor until you have crumbs.

Although the fresh and toasted varieties are somewhat interchangeable, I prefer fresh breadcrumbs when I am going to be cooking them further and toasted breadcrumbs as a finisher or topper. You can store all breadcrumbs for up to six months in the freezer and two months in your pantry (dry, cool, and out of direct sunlight).

Croutons

My *Smoky Parmesan Croutons* (page 20) are so crunchy and addictive that every time I make them my guests (usually my family) devour about half of them before the croutons get a chance to cool. And to think, just minutes before, those little crunchy cubes were *destined for the dumpster* in the form of stale bread. *I actually don't even like the term* stale bread *because it connotes an inedible state or unusable condition. Quite the contrary.*

My rule for croutons is that there is no rule. You can use just about any bread you like, crust on or off. *I prefer crust on.* You can season them with your favorite spices, spice blends, herbs, or exotic sea salts. Store your croutons in the same manner as the breadcrumbs, in an airtight container placed in a dry, cool place away from direct sunlight or place them in the freezer for up to six months. Here is a basic recipe for croutons that can be adapted to your ingredients.

Cut bread into 1-inch cubes (you can cut them into ½-inch cubes if you prefer little pebble-sized croutons). Place the bread cubes in a large bowl and add your seasoning, black pepper, and whatever dried spices you like (fresh herbs have a tendency to burn and taste bitter). Add a drizzle of extra-virgin olive oil without soaking the bread and toss until completely coated. Spread onto a baking sheet in a single layer and place in a 400°F oven for 8 minutes. Remove from the oven and sprinkle with grated Parmesan cheese if you like. *The grated cheese can burn in the oven, so add it to your freshly baked croutons immediately after removing them from the oven.*

What Else?

Throughout this book you will find recipes that utilize day-old or several-days old bread, including my hybrid creation of soufflé and quiche: *Bacon, Onion, and Olive "Souffliche"* (page 74), *Challah French Toast with Crispy Ham and Roasted Apples* (page 67), *Banana Croissant Bread Pudding with Nutella* (page 244), and gourmet grilled cheese sandwiches (pages 138 and 140).

Go to the Salvage Index and look under "Bread" to find many recipes that will turn your not-so-fresh breads into scrumptious dishes.

DRY GOODS

Have you ever opened a bag of flour or a container of oatmeal that was stored in your pantry and been horrified to find little bugs? Most dry goods are considered shelf stable, meaning the nutrition and quality of the product remains the same without refrigeration. Items such as flour, cereals, baking powder, rice, nuts, and beans will last three to six months if stored properly. This assumes you keep these items free of bugs usually by storing them out of the direct sunlight and away from moisture and heat. However, with some extra precautions and care, your dry goods can last for a year, and in some cases up to two years.

Although plastic bags and self-sealing freezer bags are an improvement over a folded up package after opening, they will not keep the bugs from eating through them. *Imagine my surprise when I opened the sealed freezer bag securing my open box of rice, only to find little weevils crawling around. How did they get in there? They eat through the plastic bag. Lesson learned.* Additionally, most grains contain insect eggs, especially organic products which are more susceptible due to the absence of pesticides. If these products are not stored properly and are exposed to moisture, sunlight, or heat, those eggs can hatch. The most effective storage practice for all dry goods is to transfer your flour, cereals, rolled oats, beans, nuts, and other items to hard plastic or glass storage containers that have a sealable lid. Sealable jars and containers will keep the moisture of the refrigerator out of the product, so you don't have to worry about the items getting clumpy should you choose to refrigerate them or store them in the freezer. You can also use glass mason jars.

Baking Powder and Baking Soda

Both of these commonly used pantry items should be stored in their original packaging. To test the effectiveness of these items, place a teaspoon of baking powder in a glass

of hot water. If it bubbles, then it is still good. For baking soda, place a teaspoon of it in a glass with vinegar. If it bubbles, it hasn't lost its potency.

Cornmeal

Cornmeal will last for up to a year in the pantry if stored in a plastic container with a sealable lid. In the refrigerator, store it in its original packaging placed in a sealable freezer bag and you can extend the shelf life an additional six months. Cornmeal in the freezer can last up to two years. As with flour, when thawing cornmeal that has been stored in the freezer, allow the product to come to room temperature in its plastic container or bag before opening.

Flour

All bags of flour should be placed in a larger freezer bag after purchase, excess air removed, and placed in the freezer for at least three days. This will help prevent the hatching of eggs and will extend the life of the product. When removing the flour from the freezer, let it come to room temperature before opening the bag. This will allow the flour to stabilize and will keep moisture from affecting the flour. Once the flour is room temperature, transfer to a hard plastic container (metal or glass is fine) with a sealable lid. It will stay fresh for up to six months, but if you don't plan on using all of it by then, store it in the refrigerator or freezer, where it will last for up to a year.

Nuts

Nuts are best stored in a cool, dry place but do best in the refrigerator. At room temperature, most nuts will last four to six weeks before going bad. When stored in a sealed container or plastic bag in the refrigerator, they will stay fresh for up to six months.

If you buy nuts in a container with a lid, you can place that sealed container directly in the refrigerator, but if you are storing in the freezer—which will extend their life for up to a year—place the closed container into a large freezer bag. When nuts give off a rancid odor, they should be thrown out.

Rice

White rice, jasmine rice, wild rice, and basmati, if properly stored, have an indefinite shelf life. Keep them free from dust and insects by storing in plastic containers with sealable lids in a dry, cool place. Brown rice has higher oil content than white rice and will spoil quicker. In the pantry, brown rice should last for three months, but you can double its shelf life by storing it in the refrigerator or freezer. A sealed plastic bag is sufficient for all storage.

Tips to avoid cross-contamination

1. Always wash your hands with soap after touching or handling proteins (meat, poultry, or fish).

2. You should also spray any countertop that has had contact with a raw protein with a disinfectant.

3. Use separate cutting boards for vegetables and proteins. Cross-contamination can happen very easily if you use, for example, the same cutting board for raw chicken as you do chopping onions.

4. Additionally, you can cross-contaminate by using the same knife, so be aware of your utensils and your surfaces any time you are dealing with a raw protein.

Fish

Fresh fish is one of those food items that is often improperly stored and mishandled. When you buy fresh fish, ask if it is in fact "fresh." You will usually get an answer like: "All our fish is fresh today," but there are ways to check for yourself. Fish should smell like the ocean, not fishy, ammonia-like, or sour. The flesh should be firm and not mushy, the surface shouldn't be oily or slimy, and when buying whole fish, the gills should be shiny and the eyes should be clear, not cloudy.

When you buy fish, keep it in the packaging or wrapping from the store until you are ready to cook it. When stored properly, fresh fish will last for two to three days in the refrigerator (under 40°F) and up to six months in the freezer (0°F). You can freeze fresh fish at any time up to the last day of freshness. Don't ever attempt to freeze fish that is beginning to smell fishy. If you are planning on keeping it in the freezer for more than two months, I would suggest you place the fish (still in its original packaging) into a sealable freezer bag or wrap with heavy-duty foil to prevent freezer burn.

There are three ways to thaw fish (and shellfish) properly. The best thawing practice is to place the fish in the refrigerator (in its packaging) on a plate and allow it to thaw slowly overnight. If you don't have the luxury of time, the second best thawing method is to place the frozen fish or shellfish in a plastic bag (if it isn't already packaged that way) and make a small cut in the bag at the corner. *This will prevent an air pocket from forming inside the bag.* Place the bag in a bowl with cold water running directly onto the fish. Turn it every few minutes and make sure the water is cold, not warm or hot. Fillets will thaw quickly and fish steaks and shrimp will take a bit longer. Lastly, if you have little or no time for proper thawing, you may use the microwave. Take the fish out of its packaging, use the defrost setting, and remove from the microwave as soon as the fish is somewhat bendable. You will have to keep an eye on this and turn the fish at least once during the defrost cycle. *I always finish by running cold water over the fish for a minute or two.* It is not recommended to refreeze fish. It isn't unsafe to do so, but the fresh qualities of the fish, including texture and flavor, will be significantly diminished.

Cooked fish can be kept in the refrigerator for two to three days in an airtight container or wrapped tightly in plastic wrap. I love to use leftover fish as a *salvage* item. Try *Mixed Fish Croquettes with Roasted Red Pepper Mayo (page 178)* or *Cod and Scallop Fritters (page 180).*

Shellfish

Fresh shellfish such as lobster, shrimp, clams, scallops, and mussels are best stored in the refrigerator for two to three days. Clams and mussels do best in a bowl covered with paper towel or a damp cloth. Live lobsters should not be kept on ice for more than a few hours and should be refrigerated in an open bowl or dish. Shrimp and scallops should be in a closed container. All shellfish can be frozen in an airtight container or wrapped tightly with plastic wrap and then heavy-duty foil and will last for up to six months. Don't ever attempt to freeze shellfish that has an off odor. Once thawed, do not refreeze; however, you can freeze them once they are cooked. Cooked shellfish can be kept in the refrigerator for one to two days.

Meat

Always keep meat in its original packaging until ready to use. Red meat and pork (steaks and chops) can be stored in the refrigerator for up to five days if the temperature is between 38° and 40°F or colder and up to year in the freezer. Raw ground meats, including beef, veal, pork, and poultry, have a shorter life span than steaks—about two to three days in the refrigerator and up to four months in the freezer. Once cooked, all meat will last about three days in the refrigerator. To freeze meat properly, place the meat in its original packaging toward the bottom of the freezer. If freezing for more than two months, place packaged meat in a sealable plastic bag. To thaw frozen meat, place in the refrigerator on a plate or in a bowl on the bottom shelf to avoid cross-contamination if the liquids spill. I don't recommend thawing in the microwave as it tends to toughen the meat.

> **Is meat that has turned brown still okay to eat?** Oxidation is a natural process and will cause the color of meat to darken. This is not a sign of spoilage. There are other indicators of meat going bad such as an off odor or a slimy or sticky surface.

Poultry

Always keep chicken and other poultry in their original packaging until ready to use. Poultry can be stored in the refrigerator for up to two days if the temperature is between 38° and 40°F or colder and up to six months in the freezer. Once cooked, poultry will last about three days in the refrigerator. To freeze poultry properly, use its original packaging and place toward the bottom of the freezer. If freezing for more than two months, place packaged poultry in a sealable plastic bag. Cooked chicken should be placed in the freezer within two hours after it is cooked. Wrap tightly with plastic wrap or heavy-duty foil or place in an airtight container. Similar to the thawing instructions for meat, thaw frozen poultry by placing in the refrigerator on a plate to avoid cross-contamination if the liquids spill. If you don't have the luxury of time, place the poultry item in a plastic bag (if it isn't already packaged that way) and make a small cut in the bag at the corner. *This will prevent an air pocket from forming inside the bag.* Place the bag in a bowl with cold water running directly over the poultry. Turn it every few minutes and make sure the water is cold, not warm or hot. Boneless chicken cutlets will thaw quickly and chicken parts or whole chickens will take a bit longer. Lastly, if you have little or no time for proper thawing, you may use the microwave. Take the poultry item out of its packaging, use the defrost setting, and remove from the microwave as soon as the poultry is somewhat bendable. You will have to keep an eye on this and turn the poultry at least once during the defrost cycle. *I like to finish by running cold water over the chicken for a minute or two.*

CHAPTER 4: RUBS, MARINADES, AND SAUCES

RUBS AND SPICES

Let's talk about all those ingredients and spices you have in your pantry and spice cabinet calling to you for attention. Have you ever bought a spice for a recipe and only used one teaspoon, leaving the entire container in your cabinet for months or years? This chapter begins with ways of utilizing many of those spices by combining them into spice blends to enhance a dish and add flavor. What I love about the blends is that you can tailor them to your taste. If you like a bit of heat, add a small pinch of cayenne pepper. Do you love rosemary? Add it to your spice blend. I utilize my spice blends in many of the recipes in this book because I personally cook with them every day as a chef at Epicure and at home when I cook for my family. Using a spice blend not only saves time, because of the wonderful flavor balance in a blend, it also keeps you from over spicing with one or more spices.

Always check your spices for freshness. As my mother used to say, "The nose knows." Check all spice containers that have been opened for six months or longer by smelling them. They should have a distinctive spice flavor. Also, look closely for little bugs that can hatch after the spice has been stored for a long time.

ALL-PURPOSE LOVE RUB

My absolute favorite spice blend is my All-Purpose Love Rub. Michele and I literally use this blend every time we cook at home, and the meat department in Epicure's three stores have adopted it has their go-to rub and overall seasoning. I love smoked paprika and I seem to sneak it into all of my rubs. Its smoky earthy aroma combines well with dried herbs such as oregano, thyme, and basil and pairs perfectly with powdered or dehydrated garlic with its salty bite.

Makes 3 cups

1½ cups salt
¾ cup smoked paprika
½ cup garlic powder
3 tablespoons black pepper
2 tablespoons white pepper
2 tablespoons dried basil
2 teaspoons cayenne pepper
   (optional)

PLACE ALL INGREDIENTS into a medium-sized bowl. Mix the spices together with a fork until blended. Transfer into a plastic container with a sealable lid or a glass jar with a lid.

Creative uses . . .

- *This spice blend is excellent as a rub on steaks. Sprinkle the blend generously on all sides of the meat, place steaks in a resealable plastic, and refrigerate for 30 minutes to overnight. Pan sear, grill, or broil.*
- *For a delicious roasted chicken, rub the skin with 2 tablespoons of spice blend and 2 tablespoons of olive oil. Roast the chicken on a vertical chicken roaster or sit the chicken on a metal canister like a half full beer can.*
- *Season your fish with the spice blend and squeeze half a lemon or lime with a drizzle of olive oil before grilling, baking, broiling, or pan searing.*
- *Use this spice blend on all your salads. Either blend it into your salad dressing or sprinkle a teaspoon over your salad before tossing.*
- *I love using this blend as a seasoning on sandwiches. Sprinkle it on your sandwich in place of salt and pepper, or blend with a tablespoon of mayonnaise for a flavorful mayo.*
- *One of the best snacks for the family is "love rubbed popcorn." If popping your own popped corn, add a tablespoon of the All Purpose Love Rub to the oil before adding the kernels. You can also sprinkle the Love Rub on freshly popped corn.*
- *"The Love Scramble" is one of my favorite egg dishes. Simply add 1 teaspoon for every egg used in your scrambled eggs or omelet.*
- *If you like the combination of salty and sweet, sprinkle this blend on your favorite ice cream. Especially good on vanilla bean ice cream!*

CHILI SPICE BLEND

This blend is slightly spicy and is the perfect seasoning to prepare chili. Simply add two tablespoons of Chili Spice Blend per pound of meat.

Makes 1 cup

¼ cup chili powder
2 tablespoons ground cumin
2 tablespoons ground
   coriander
2 tablespoons dried oregano
2 tablespoons smoked
   paprika
1 tablespoon cayenne
   pepper
1 tablespoon salt
1 tablespoon black pepper

PLACE ALL INGREDIENTS into a medium-sized bowl. Mix the spices together with a fork until blended. Transfer into a plastic container with a sealable lid or a glass jar with a lid.

Creative uses . . .

- *If you are using beans in your chili, add an additional tablespoon of the spice blend.*
- *A great way to salvage leftover ground beef, chicken, or turkey is to reheat the meat with a tablespoon of spice blend.*
- *For a cool and spicy dip, try mixing a tablespoon into plain Greek yogurt.*
- *Sprinkle this blend on cooked rice, add white or red beans, and any chopped cooked leftover vegetables.*
- *Similar to the Love Rub, you can add the Chili Spice Blend to mayonnaise for a delicious spread for sandwiches.*

SAVORY SPICE BLEND

This savory blend is filled with Mediterranean flavors and is fantastic on steaks, burgers, pork, and chicken.

Makes 1 cup

3 tablespoons ground cumin
2 tablespoons salt
2 tablespoons smoked paprika
1 tablespoon garlic powder
1 tablespoon onion powder
1 tablespoon ground coriander
1 tablespoon dried oregano
1 tablespoon cayenne pepper
1 tablespoon sweet paprika
1 tablespoon black pepper

PLACE ALL INGREDIENTS into a medium-sized bowl. Mix the spices together with a fork until blended. Transfer into a plastic container with a sealable lid or a glass jar with a lid.

Creative uses . . .

- *I love this spice blend with rice, particularly with quinoa and risotto (use a teaspoon of spice blend for every cup of cooked rice).*
- *A great way to make use of leftover rice (white or brown) is to combine chickpeas, capers, and chopped olives along with a generous sprinkle of spice blend.*
- *Try a savory omelet with 2 teaspoons of this spice blend and ¼ cup of crumbled feta.*
- *Make a delicious cold or hot pasta dish by adding 1 tablespoon of Savory Spice Blend to one pound of pasta (I prefer bowtie or penne), along with chopped roasted red peppers, artichoke hearts, and grated Parmesan or crumbled feta.*
- *Kick up the flavor of tomato or chicken soup with a teaspoon of this spice blend.*
- *To use up the last bit of sour cream or plain yogurt, add spice blend and use on everything from soups and stews, roasted chicken, grilled fish, and all cooked vegetables.*

SOUTHERN SPICE BLEND

This blend works well on many traditional southern recipes including vegetables, meats, and soups and is fantastic as a dry rub on pork. The touch of cinnamon gives the blend a unique spicy note.

Makes 1 cup

3 tablespoons ground cumin
2 tablespoons salt
2 tablespoons smoked
   paprika
1 tablespoon garlic powder
1 tablespoon onion powder
1 tablespoon ground
   coriander
1 tablespoon dried oregano
1 tablespoon cayenne
   pepper
1 tablespoon sweet paprika
1 tablespoon black pepper
2 teaspoons cinnamon

PLACE ALL INGREDIENTS into a medium-sized bowl. Mix the spices together with a fork until blended. Transfer into a plastic container with a sealable lid or a glass jar with a lid.

Creative uses . . .

- *For the best fried chicken, add this spice blend to your dredging flour.*
- *Add to canned tuna with a drizzle of olive oil and chopped cilantro or parsley.*
- *Add to soups with a dollop of sour cream.*
- *Combine the spice blend with plain yogurt for a spicy southern-inspired dip.*
- *Mix into pancake batter with sautéed red peppers and onions. Drop tablespoons of batter into hot vegetable or canola oil for fabulous fritters.*

BBQ SPICE BLEND

Everyone loves great barbeque. This blend can be used to make a delicious BBQ sauce (page 51), but also is perfect as a rub on chicken, beef, and especially pork.

Makes 1½ cups

½ cup light brown sugar
¼ cup powdered garlic
2 tablespoons dried thyme
2 tablespoons powdered onion
2 tablespoons dry mustard
2 tablespoons smoked paprika
2 tablespoons black pepper
2 teaspoons ground cumin
2 teaspoons sweet paprika
1 teaspoon cayenne pepper

PLACE ALL INGREDIENTS into a medium-sized bowl. Mix the spices together with a fork until blended. Transfer into a plastic container with a sealable lid or a glass jar with a lid.

Creative uses . . .

- *Sprinkle on roasted potatoes and serve with plain yogurt or sour cream.*
- *For the most delicious homemade french fries, toss freshly cut potatoes with a generous amount of spice blend, a drizzle of vegetable oil, and bake for 40 minutes.*
- *Rub on pork chops and sear quickly, followed by 10 minutes in a 350°F oven.*
- *Sprinkle on bacon and roast in the oven until crispy.*
- *Mix with chopped hard-boiled eggs and a touch of mayonnaise.*

SPANISH SPICE BLEND

This spice blend is the base flavor for my Chorizo Ginger Broth (page 173). Use it whenever you want to add a Spanish kick to your dishes.

Makes 1½ cups

2 tablespoons powdered garlic
1 tablespoon powdered onion
1 tablespoon ground cumin
1 tablespoon sweet paprika
2 tablespoons smoked paprika
1 tablespoon dried thyme
1 tablespoon dried oregano
2 tablespoons salt
1 tablespoon black pepper
1 teaspoon cayenne pepper

PLACE ALL INGREDIENTS into a medium-sized bowl. Mix the spices together with a fork until blended. Transfer into a plastic container with a sealable lid or a glass jar with a lid.

Creative uses . . .

- *As with other spice blends, add the Southern Spice Blend to rice. For a fabulous, classic Latin rice dish, combine the spice blend with sautéed onion, celery, and chorizo.*
- *Sprinkle a tablespoon of spice blend to ground beef, turkey, or chicken and top with melted Manchego for a savory spicy burger.*
- *A delicious side dish with a Latin flair combines pinto beans or black beans, spice blend, and a tablespoon of chopped parsley or cilantro while heating.*

SWEET AND SPICED SPICE BLEND

This blend combines many of your infrequently used spices that are still flavorful. Try it on ice cream, pancakes and waffles, and buttered or french toast. The addition of salt brings out all the flavors.

Makes ¾ cup

½ cup granulated sugar
2 tablespoons cinnamon
1 tablespoon allspice
2 teaspoons salt
½ teaspoon nutmeg
½ teaspoon ground ginger
¼ teaspoon ground cloves

PLACE ALL INGREDIENTS into a medium-sized bowl. Mix the spices together with a fork until blended. Transfer into a plastic container with a sealable lid or a glass jar with a lid.

MARINADES

The base for many popular marinades contains oil (olive, canola, vegetable), an acidic component such as wine, vinegar, lemon or lime juice, dried or fresh herbs, and shallots, onions, and/or garlic. There are several factors that determine the type of marinade to use and how long the food item should soak in the liquid. Use an oil-based marinade for lean or dry meat, a marinade with an acidic base such as lemon juice, wine, or vinegar for meats that need tenderizing or a combination of oil and acidity for additional flavor and tenderizing.

Marinating overnight is recommended for large or thick cuts of meat such as a pork shoulder, beef roasts, and bone-in poultry. As in all salvage preparations, use ingredients on hand and lead with your favorite flavors.

Marinating Poultry

For boneless chicken or turkey breasts and thighs, this marinade will permeate the poultry in as little as 20 minutes but works best in the refrigerator for 4 to 6 hours or overnight if you have the time. For chicken or turkey parts on the bone, marinate for at least an hour or overnight to penetrate the flesh and tenderize.

The best technique is to pour marinade into a large plastic sealable freezer bag. Place your chicken pieces into the bag and remove as much of the excess air as possible before sealing. Once sealed, gently squeeze the bag to massage the chicken and distribute the marinade into every crevice of the chicken. Place bag in the refrigerator.

Marinating Beef and Pork

Marinating meats, including steaks, chops, and roasts, adds flavor, helps create a good sear on the outside of the meat, and tenderizes as well. The acidic component does the tenderizing and, for leaner cuts, the oil adds fat for juiciness. It is best to have the marinade work its magic overnight when dealing with a roast, thick-cut chop, or pork loin. If overnight marinating isn't possible, 30 minutes will greatly improve the end result, especially steaks of medium thickness.

Marinating Fish

Marinating fish takes a bit more attention than meat or poultry due to its tender flesh. The acidity that vinegar, wine, or citrus brings to a marinade can actually "cook" the fish if left in it too long. Marinating fish not only imparts flavor, but the oil in the marinade can also keep it moist and help prevent the fish from sticking.

Firm fish like tuna, swordfish, and halibut can take a marinade for up to 2 hours if cut thick (1½ to 2-inches thick) and from 30 minutes to 1 hour for a thinner fillet. Flakey fish like flounder, cod, and salmon can marinate from 10 to 30 minutes. Use the flavors you like or have in your kitchen. I like to use rosemary instead of thyme, substitute white wine for lemon juice, shallots for garlic, etc. The key to successful salvage in the kitchen is taking advantage of what you have and being flexible with the ingredients.

All of these marinades can be used as a salad dressing as well!

- Food items do not have to be completely submerged in marinade.

- You can use a glass baking dish or shallow bowl to marinate larger items, but for chicken breasts, pork chops, and smaller cuts, I prefer a large plastic sealable freezer bag.

- Brush on marinades with a pastry brush to cover all the surfaces of the meat, chicken, or fish. Leave a small amount of the marinade in the bottom of your dish or bowl. Refrigerate from 20 minutes to overnight.

- Once meat, chicken, or fish is cooked, do **not** use the marinade for basting or any other purpose, as you run the risk of contamination from bacteria.

- Wash your hands thoroughly with soap after handling meat, chicken, or fish.

HERBS AND OLIVE OIL MARINADE

This is my "go to" marinade for all types of meat and fish, whether I am grilling, broiling, or pan searing. The egg white helps pull the marinade together.

Makes about 1½ cups

½ cup olive oil
3 ounces orange juice
1 lime, juiced
1 egg white
2 garlic cloves, peeled and
   crushed
1 tablespoon shallots,
   minced
½ cup fresh herbs, chopped
   (basil, oregano, rosemary,
   thyme, chervil, dill, parsley,
   or sage)
1 teaspoon salt
1 teaspoon black pepper
1 teaspoon *All-Purpose
   Love Rub* (page 29),
   optional

USING A BLENDER or food processor, pulse all the ingredients (except oil) until blended. At a low speed, slowly drizzle half the oil until marinade begins to emulsify. Turn to high speed and add the rest of the oil all at once. Add salt and pepper and pulse a few times to blend.

Taste for seasoning.

Creative uses . . .

- *You can substitute shallots, red onions, or white onions for the garlic.*
- *Any fresh or not-so-fresh herbs will do as long as they still retain their green color and haven't become slimy. Their aroma should be clean and fragrant. I like dill, parsley, and chervil together. Or cilantro, parsley, and thyme. Go with what you have and what you prefer.*
- *Any citrus juice will work perfectly in this marinade. You can also combine several citrus fruits such as grapefruit, lemon, and orange juice (also use the zests for additional flavor).*
- *The addition of a teaspoon of Dijon mustard transforms the marinade into a fabulous salad dressing.*
- *When grilling, use this to baste your meat, poultry, or fish.*

SWEET AND SPICY GRILLING MARINADE

My grandmother's cook, Louise, used ginger ale on her baked ham because the sugar in the soda would caramelize. This marinade uses Coke, but you can use any soda you have. It's good even if the soda has gone flat, as the carbonation serves no purpose in the marinade. Lemons, oranges, or grapefruits can be used in place of limes. You can marinade beef, pork, and chicken before cooking and you can also brush it on when grilling.

Makes 2 cups

1 cup vegetable oil
6 ounces soda
2 limes, juiced
3 tablespoons *BBQ Spice Blend* (page 34)
2 tablespoons ketchup
1 tablespoon Worcestershire sauce
1 tablespoon salt
2 garlic cloves, peeled and minced
¼ teaspoon hot sauce

WHISK TOGETHER all ingredients (except oil) in a small bowl until combined. Whisk in the oil. Taste for seasoning.

Creative uses . . .

- *Add marinade to sea bass, salmon, or tuna in a sealed freezer bag. Refrigerate for one hour. Take out of refrigerator and let come to room temperature before grilling. Use additional marinade (that hasn't had contact with the protein) to brush on after one side of the fish is cooked.*
- *Marinate uncooked chicken strips overnight and bake in the oven for 20 minutes until cooked through. Serve with a sprinkle of BBQ Spice Blend (page 34).*
- *Place a pork loin in a small roasting pan, cover with a generous amount of marinade, cover with plastic wrap, and place in refrigerator overnight. Remove plastic wrap and roast in 400°F oven for 30 to 40 minutes, until slightly pink in the middle. Serve with sliced pineapples.*

ASIAN GINGER MARINADE

I love this marinade because, aside from the water, every ingredient is a salvage ingredient. Every time I buy soy sauce, chili sauce, or sweet chili garlic sauce, once opened, it sits in my refrigerator for months. This is a great way to utilize these opened condiments and has many delicious uses. Additionally, this is a good use for your brown or white sugar that has become hard and clumpy as the sugar will dissolve in water.

Makes 3 cups

½ cup water
2 tablespoons brown sugar
2 tablespoons granulated
   sugar
1 teaspoon ground ginger
1½ cups chili garlic sauce
   (usually bottled and can
   be found in most gourmet
   or Asian markets)
½ cup chili sauce
2 tablespoons soy sauce

PLACE A SMALL POT with water, sugars, and ground ginger over a medium heat. Stir and bring to a simmer. Add the chili garlic sauce, chili sauce, and soy sauce to the pot and continue simmering for 10 minutes, stirring frequently while the sauce thickens.

REMOVE FROM THE HEAT and allow to cool. Taste for seasoning.

Creative uses . . .

- *This marinade makes a delicious glaze on chicken wings and drum sticks.*
- *Use as a marinade on duck or pork and brush on the cooked meat as a finishing glaze.*
- *My favorite use for the marinade is Asian Ginger Salmon (page 170). You don't need to marinate the salmon. Simply pour or brush the marinade onto the salmon (not the skin) and roast in the oven for no more than 8 to 10 minutes.*
- *In addition to marinating, the mixture works as a fine dipping sauce for fried appetizers such as fritters or chicken wings.*

JERK CHICKEN MARINADE

Jerk chicken and jerk pork recipes have become popular across the country. The Caribbean flavor combination of sweet, spicy, and savory works well on slow cooked and grilled meats. My Sweet and Spicy Spice Blend in combination with the heat of the peppers make the perfect Jamaican-inspired marinade that also works with beef, pork, turkey, and duck.

Makes about 1½ cups

½ red onion, finely chopped
2 garlic cloves, minced
1 shallot, finely chopped
1 Serrano pepper, seeded and finely chopped (or use 2 dried red chilies if available)
¼ cup soy sauce
2 tablespoons fresh thyme (leaves only), chopped, or 2 teaspoons dried thyme
3 tablespoons *Sweet and Spiced Spice Blend* (page 36)
3 tablespoons canola oil
2 tablespoons cider vinegar (or white wine vinegar)
1 teaspoon black pepper

USING A BLENDER or food processor, pulse all the ingredients until well blended.

TASTE FOR SEASONING.

MEXICAN PORK MARINADE

Savory Spice Blend is the base note for this marinade and uses the acidity from the red wine vinegar to break down the meat and make it super tender. If you want more heat, add ½ teaspoon of cayenne pepper or a few drops of hot sauce to the marinade.

Makes just over 1 cup

3 ounces red wine vinegar
¼ cup *Steak Sauce* (page 57)
½ cup grape seed oil (can substitute vegetable or canola)
2 tablespoons *Savory Spice Blend* (page 32)
2 garlic cloves, peeled and crushed
1 teaspoon salt

WHISK TOGETHER all the ingredients until well blended. Taste for seasoning.

Creative uses . . .

- *I absolutely love this as a dressing. Especially spooned generously over freshly cut tomatoes and red onion slices.*
- *This marinade is delicious over a juicy steak or pork chop.*
- *Mix with ½ cup of apple sauce and serve with turkey or ham on the holidays.*
- *Marinate a boneless turkey breast (4 to 5 pounds) overnight for a delicious turkey London broil. Simply broil each side for 4 to 5 minutes and then turn the heat down to 350°F and finish cooking for 20 minutes.*

LEMON-LIME ROSEMARY MARINADE

This is my favorite marinade for pork loin and grilled fish. You don't have to use both lemon and lime, but if you have them, use them. Dried rosemary can be substituted for fresh, just remember to use one-third the amount of dried. You can also substitute thyme for the rosemary.

Makes 1 cup

½ cup olive oil
3 garlic cloves, smashed and
  roughly chopped
1 lemon, juiced (plus
  ½ teaspoon of zest)
1 lime, juiced (plus
  ½ teaspoon of zest)
2 sprigs fresh rosemary
  (leaves only), finely
  chopped
1 teaspoon salt
1 teaspoon black pepper
1 teaspoon dry mustard

WHISK TOGETHER all the ingredients until well blended. Taste for seasoning.

Creative uses . . .
- *Pour over jasmine rice and baby peas for a deliciously tangy side dish.*
- *Marinate your chicken parts overnight when planning a daytime BBQ.*
- *My favorite use of this marinade is grilled swordfish. Simply add marinade to fish for about 30 minutes before grilling and brush the marinade on the cooked side of the fish. The citrus will begin the cooking process so your grilling time will be short, about 3 to 4 minutes on the first side and 1 to 2 minutes for side two.*

HAWAIIAN FISH MARINADE

This fish marinade combines tanginess from the orange juice and cider vinegar, a salty bite of the garlic powder, soy sauce, and fish sauce, and slightly sweet notes from the honey and ginger. Use it for light flaky fish or thick cut firm fish.

Makes 1 cup

5 ounces olive oil
½ cup orange juice
2 tablespoons cider vinegar
2 tablespoons soy sauce
1 tablespoon honey
2 teaspoons ground ginger
2 teaspoons garlic powder
¼ teaspoon fish sauce
3 sprigs fresh thyme
   (leaves only)
1 teaspoon white pepper

WHISK TOGETHER all ingredients until well blended. Taste for seasoning.

Creative uses . . .
- *Add cut up pineapple and an extra sprinkle of salt for an added kick.*
- *When you're in the mood for a stir-fry, cook your protein and vegetables first, and then pour in about ½ cup of the marinade. Stir together and serve with Asian noodles or leftover rice.*
- *Dice ¼ cup each of red and yellow bell pepper and add to marinade. Use on top of grilled fish or chicken. I love this version on top of freshly shucked clams and oysters.*

SAUCES

I love combining salvage ingredients with fresh ingredients to create a sauce that enhances and embraces the food I prepare. The Everything Sauce and Pesto Sauce are simple blender sauces, while the Gruyère, Cheddar, and Bleu Cheese Sauce utilizes a classic béchamel preparation. The BBQ Sauce, Steak Sauce, and Tomato Sauce are slower reduction types of sauces.

EVERYTHING SAUCE

I've called this sauce my Everything Sauce because it's prepared from a little bit of this and a little bit of that. It is the perfect partner for literally everything from pasta and rice to chicken, fish, pork, and steak, over steamed vegetables as well as a salad dressing, and it also tastes great on sandwiches. This sauce is a great way to use up that last yogurt in the refrigerator, the last bit of mayo and capers at the bottom of the jar, and your fresh herbs before they go bad. You can use only yogurt if you want to lower the calories and fat.

Makes about 1½ cups

½ cup mayonnaise
½ cup plain yogurt
¼ cup fresh herbs (dill, thyme, sage, rosemary, parsley, oregano), roughly chopped
2 tablespoons capers
2 anchovies
½ lime, juiced and zested
2 teaspoons dried cumin
2 teaspoons ground coriander
2 teaspoons red chili flakes
2 teaspoons salt

BLEND TOGETHER all ingredients in a food processor or blender. Taste for seasoning.

Refrigerate in a sealed container for up to two weeks.

PESTO SAUCE

My son Miles's favorite pasta sauce is pesto. I like combining fresh parsley and basil as I find straight basil a bit too "grassy." If I have on hand, I will use equal amounts of Parmesan and Romano. A simpler French variation is to make your pesto without pine nuts. You can freeze fresh pesto in an air tight container or keep for up to two weeks in the refrigerator if you add a small layer of olive oil on top (1 tablespoon).

Makes about ¾ cup

1 garlic clove, crushed
¼ cup pine nuts
½ teaspoon salt (Kosher is
    best)
1 cup fresh basil, rinsed and
    dried
1 cup parsley, rinsed and
    dried
2 tablespoons Parmesan,
    grated
2 tablespoons Pecorino
    Romano, grated
¼ cup olive oil

PLACE A DRY PAN on medium-low heat and add pine nuts. Shake pan back and forth every 20 to 30 seconds so pine nuts lightly toast. This will take about 2 minutes.

MAKE THE PESTO by combining garlic, toasted pine nuts, and salt in a small food processor. Pulse until a chunky paste forms. Add basil, parsley, cheeses, and oil. Pulse until smooth but still chunky. Taste for seasoning.

MICHAEL'S SMOKY SINGLE MALT BBQ SAUCE

This recipe invades not only your spice cabinet but also your liquor cabinet. I like the smokiness of single malt scotch but you can use any blended whiskey or bourbon or leave it out altogether. The alcohol burns off so you don't have to worry about anyone getting tipsy from too much BBQ sauce. What makes this recipe easy to prepare is the use of the spice blend. For a little more heat, add ½ teaspoon of cayenne pepper or add a teaspoon of hot sauce.

Makes 2½ cups

1 tablespoon olive oil
¼ pound bacon (about 3 to 4 strips), cut into ½-inch strips
½ onion, finely chopped
4 garlic cloves, peeled and minced
1 tablespoon cider vinegar
¼ cup single malt scotch
1½ cups ketchup
3 tablespoons Dijon mustard
2 tablespoons Worcestershire sauce
2 tablespoons honey
¼ cup *BBQ Spice Blend* (page 34)
Salt

IN A LARGE SAUTÉ PAN over medium-high heat, add oil until shimmering. Add bacon strips and onion and cook for 8 minutes until onions soften and bacon is crispy. Add garlic, stir, and cook for another minute.

AWAY FROM THE FLAME, add the vinegar and scotch. Reduce for 2 minutes while alcohol evaporates. Add ketchup, Worcestershire sauce, honey, and spice blend. Stir well and lower the heat. Simmer for 15 minutes. Taste for seasoning. The addition of salt will bring out the flavors.

GRUYÈRE, CHEDDAR, AND BLEU CHEESE SAUCE

The base for this sauce is a basic white sauce and infuses the flavors of the herbs you have on hand. I like to use thyme and garlic but I will gladly use a shallot or green onion and rosemary or sage, if that's what I have. You can be creative in blending the cheeses. Simply remove the rind, cut away any dried portion of the cheese, and cut into cubes. It is always best to use a larger quantity of the mildest cheese and a lesser amount of the sharpest or strongest cheese.

Makes 3 cups

- 2 cups milk
- 1 sprig thyme
- 2 cloves garlic, unpeeled and smashed
- 2 tablespoons unsalted butter
- 2 tablespoons all-purpose flour
- 1 cup sharp cheddar, shredded
- ½ cup Gruyère shredded
- ¼ cup bleu cheese, crumbled
- 1 tablespoon parsley, chopped, or use 2 teaspoons dried parsley
- 1 teaspoon black pepper
- Salt

GENTLY HEAT THE MILK, thyme, and garlic in a small saucepan over a medium heat. Lightly simmer for 5 minutes to infuse flavors, but do not boil. Set aside.

MELT BUTTER in a skillet over medium-high heat. Using a wooden spoon, stir in flour, and cook for 1 to 2 minutes. Stir constantly to keep lumps from forming. Adjust the temperature so the roux does not brown.

PLACE A STRAINER OVER THE SKILLET and slowly pour the warm milk into the flour mixture. Increase heat to medium-high and whisk vigorously to dissolve any lumps. Continue whisking as sauce thickens, about 5 more minutes.

STIR IN THE CHEESES, parsley, black pepper, and continue to cook until smooth. Taste the sauce and add salt to your liking.

More possibilities . . .

- *The best way to test your blend of cheeses is to try small amounts together on a plain cracker. This will give you an idea of the balance of flavors and help you determine the proportions that suit your taste.*
- *Use this cheese sauce over any kind of pasta, including Bacon, Truffle, 4-Cheese Mac 'n' Cheese (page 222)*
- *Pour over cooked vegetables and serve, or place veggies and cheese sauce in a casserole dish, sprinkle with breadcrumbs and your favorite spice blend, and bake for 10 minutes.*
- *Stir in ½ cup of white wine for fondue.*
- *Add cheese sauce to cooked ground beef for delicious nachos.*

THE BEST BASIC TOMATO SAUCE

There are thousands of recipes for tomato sauce. My preference is a combination of fresh Roma tomatoes that have been slow roasted in the oven with canned San Marzano tomatoes. Use any variety of tomatoes and don't worry if they have become soft or bruised. A hint of fresh basil, bay leaf, garlic, some heat from dried chilies, and a pinch of sugar round out my basic sauce. You can go with a spicier version by increasing the amount of red chili flake. The red wine is optional.

Makes about 3 pints of sauce

ROASTED TOMATOES (Makes 2 cups)

2 pounds tomatoes, cut in half
1 teaspoon salt
1 teaspoon pepper
2 tablespoons olive oil
4 to 5 sprigs fresh thyme

TOMATO SAUCE

2 tablespoons olive oil
1 teaspoon red chili flakes
1 onion
4 garlic cloves, peeled

1 cup red wine
1 cup *Roasted Tomatoes* (see recipe below)
1 (28-ounce) can whole San Marzano tomatoes, crushed by hand
1 teaspoon dried oregano
¼ cup fresh basil (about 4 to 6 leaves), roughly chopped
1 bay leaf
Pinch of sugar
Salt and black pepper

ROASTED TOMATOES

PREHEAT OVEN TO 275°F. Place tomatoes, salt, pepper, oil, and thyme in a small bowl and toss to combine. Lay tomatoes on a baking sheet, cut-side down. Drizzle ingredients from the bowl evenly over the tomatoes. Slow roast for 2 hours until slightly charred and caramelized.

TOMATO SAUCE

HEAT 2 TABLESPOONS OF OIL in a pan over medium heat. Add chili flakes and garlic cloves and press the cloves down with the back of spoon. When garlic begins to brown, add onions and toss to coat with olive oil. Continue cooking until onions are slightly translucent, about 5 minutes. Add wine to deglaze. Reduce liquid by half.

ADD ROASTED TOMATOES, canned tomatoes, oregano, half the basil, bay leaf, and sugar. Bring to a simmer and cook for 15 minutes to thicken.

TASTE THE SAUCE, season with salt and black pepper. Add the remaining fresh basil and give the sauce a stir. Remove from heat to cool. Place in an airtight container and refrigerate up to two weeks. You can freeze the sauce for up to six months.

Creative uses . . .

- *A handful of fresh chopped herbs you have on hand is a great way to finish this sauce.*
- *Add chopped olives, capers, and anchovies either when cooking the onions (for a strong savory sauce) or when adding the tomatoes (for a more subtle flavor enhancement) for a Puttanesca-style sauce.*
- *Sliced peppers and red onions make a nice sweet addition. Add them in place of the onions and omit the sugar.*
- *For a bold pasta sauce, add some ground sausage to the oil along with the garlic. When sausage is cooked through, add the onions. I like lots of fresh cracked black pepper in this sauce.*
- *For a smooth tomato sauce, you can blend this sauce in the blender or food processor.*

STEAK SAUCE

Although I usually enjoy the flavor of steak with no accompaniment, this steak sauce is addictive over a NY strip, can be used to make a savory marinade (Mexican Pork Marinade, page 45), or as a base for a tangy salad dressing. This steak sauce is not as sweet as the famous Peter Luger sauce and less vinegary than the classic A1.

Makes about 1½ cups

1 medium onion, sliced
2 garlic cloves, crushed
½ cup ketchup
¼ cup honey
2 tablespoons cider vinegar
2 tablespoons soy sauce
2 tablespoons
   Worcestershire sauce
2 teaspoons dry mustard
1 teaspoon ground ginger
1 teaspoon whole allspice
   berries or dried allspice
1 lemon, juiced
Salt

COMBINE ALL INGREDIENTS in a medium pot. Bring to a boil then lower the heat and simmer for 20 minutes, stirring occasionally while the sauce thickens.

STRAIN to remove the onions, garlic, and allspice berries. Taste for seasoning.
   Keep refrigerated.

Creative uses . . .
- *Try this tangy savory sauce as a glaze on chicken thighs, baked in the oven.*
- *Add a tablespoon to sautéed vegetables for a tangy side dish.*
- *I love a tablespoon of this sauce mixed into leftover brown rice and cooked broccoli.*
- *This sauce is terrific condiment for backyard BBQs. Try it on hotdogs and hamburgers in place of ketchup.*

VANILLA BOURBON SAUCE

What can you pour a delicious velvety vanilla sauce over? Everything. Obviously bread pudding just wouldn't be the same without a decadent sauce, but this version is amazing on just about any dessert. The crucial ingredient in this sauce is the vanilla. Make sure you buy the best, it's worth it.

Makes about 1 cup

1 tablespoon butter
3 tablespoons light brown sugar
1 tablespoon granulated sugar
1 tablespoon cornstarch
½ teaspoon ground cinnamon
¼ teaspoon ground nutmeg
½ teaspoon salt
¾ cup whole milk
1 tablespoon bourbon
1 tablespoon pure vanilla extract

MELT THE BUTTER in a medium pot. Add both sugars and stir until dissolved. Add cornstarch, cinnamon, nutmeg, and salt and give a stir to combine.

WHISK IN THE MILK slowly. Add the bourbon and simmer for 5 minutes, continuing to whisk while the alcohol burns off and the sauce thickens.

REMOVE FROM THE HEAT and allow to cool. Stir in the vanilla and add salt to taste.

> The best vanilla is **pure vanilla extract,** not vanilla flavor or imitation vanilla.

Creative uses . . .

- *If you like almond flavor or any other extract that you have on hand, use it in place of the vanilla to create your favorite sauce.*
- *Pour over ice cream and freshly whipped cream.*
- *Take brownies and cookies to another level of delicious with a drizzle of warm sauce.*
- *I love this sauce over fresh blueberries, fresh fruit, warm muffins, sponge cake, and a bowl of plain Greek yogurt with sliced bananas.*

MIXED FRUIT COULIS

Makes 1 cup

1½ cups mixed fruit
½ cup granulated sugar
¼ cup water
½ lemon, juiced

PLACE MIXED FRUIT, granulated sugar, water, and lemon juice into a medium pot over high heat. Bring to a boil, then lower the heat to a simmer for 10 minutes. Remove from heat and let cool completely.

FOR A LESS CHUNKY SAUCE, pour cooled mixture into a blender and purée.

FOR A COULIS, strain the hot mixture.
    Refrigerate for up to two weeks.

Next to bread, the most thrown out food item is fruit. When fruit is over-ripe, it isn't very appetizing, except when you transform it into a sauce. A fruit coulis is cooked down fruit with sugar that is strained into a light sauce. You can leave out the last step of straining to create a chunky fruit sause.

CHAPTER 5: REASONS TO RISE

Dishes for Breakfast and Lunch

EGGS

Eggs are not only the most common ingredient in breakfast and lunch dishes worldwide, but are also an amazing salvage facilitator. There is literally no end to the fantastic combinations of leftovers and vegetables that can be added to scrambled eggs to make a healthy, satisfying, cost saving, and salvaging meal. Experiment with the variety of the contents from your produce drawer to add to crepes, pancakes, waffles, omelets, quiches, soufflés, and my favorite, frittatas. I've created a souffliche (soufflé and quiche) you can prepare based on your tastes and whatever leftover or excess items you have in your refrigerator.

Other ingredients like several-days old bread, boiled or baked potatoes, sun-dried tomatoes, anchovies, capers, roasted red peppers, and ends of cheese can be individually featured or used in combination with any of the egg recipes in this chapter. Fresh herbs, grated Parmesan cheese and your favorite spice blend can help you transform ordinary dishes and leftovers into delicious surprises.

HOW DO I TELL IF MY EGGS ARE STILL GOOD?

Eggs have a shelf life of about one month. Store-bought eggs have an expiration date and in most cases will be safe for a short time after that date. The best storage practice is to keep the eggs in the original carton and place in the middle of the refrigerator. I don't recommend taking the eggs out of their original carton or packaging and placing them in the plastic egg tray located on the refrigerator door. The door temperature can be 5 to 10° higher than the middle of the refrigerator and will shorten the shelf life of your eggs significantly.

If you aren't sure if your eggs are fresh enough, there are several tests. The first is the open egg test. Crack one open and see if there are any off odors. If the yolk is flat and not sitting up in the albumen (egg white) or if it has a cloudy appearance, don't use it. The second test is the slosh test. Gently shake an egg close to your ear. If you hear a sloshing sound, toss it. Lastly, the most accurate is the water test. Place an egg in a bowl of water. If it sinks to the bottom, it's fresh, about a week old. If it sinks to the bottom but tips slightly upward, it's about two to three weeks old, still safe to consume. If the egg bobs under the surface with just the tip breaking the surface, it's about three to four weeks old and still okay. If it floats to the top, throw it away. This happens because there is a small pocket of air inside the egg that increases in size over the course of four to five weeks from when it was laid.

Hard boiled eggs will stay fresh in the refrigerator for up to seven days if wrapped in plastic wrap or placed in an airtight container. I don't recommend freezing whole eggs, raw or hard boiled, although if you have leftover egg yolks (from using the whites), you can blend the egg yolks and freeze in an airtight container.

CHALLAH FRENCH TOAST
with Crispy Ham and Roasted Apples

Challah bread, egg bread, or brioche is the best for french toast. My mother, my sister, and I have been making it with challah bread since I can remember; my twist on the classic method is the smear of honey. Use your own creativity with the stacking of the bread slices, apples, and ham. Any apple on hand will do. If your apples are bruised, simply cut away those areas, as the rest of the apple will be fine. Your french toast will be better if the bread is slightly dried out. Challah is best because of the slight sweetness and the delicate smooth crust.

Serves 2

4 slices ham, thinly sliced
Black pepper
1 apple, cored, quartered
  and sliced to ½-inch
  wedges
4 tablespoons butter (2
  tablespoons melted for the
  apples)
¼ cup maple syrup
1 teaspoon cinnamon
3 eggs
¼ cup milk
1 tablespoon heavy cream
½ teaspoon pure vanilla
  extract
Salt
4 slices of day old challah
  bread, sliced 1½ to 2-
  inches thick
1 tablespoon honey
1 cup assorted fresh fruit for
  garnish
1 tablespoon confectioners'
  sugar (powdered sugar)

PREHEAT OVEN TO 400°F.

LAY THE SLICES OF HAM on a piece of foil, coarsely grind 1 teaspoon of black pepper over them, and place in the oven until crispy, about 8 minutes. You can use a baking or cookie sheet.

IN A SMALL BOWL, toss apples, 2 tablespoons melted butter, maple syrup, and ½ teaspoon of cinnamon until well coated. Pour contents of bowl into a small roasting pan and place in the oven for 10 minutes (at the same time as the ham). Apples should be soft and caramelized.

WHISK EGGS, MILK, CREAM, vanilla, remaining ½ teaspoon cinnamon, and a pinch of salt in a shallow glass baking dish until well combined and foamy. Soak challah slices on both sides in the egg mixture until liquid is mostly absorbed.

MELT 2 TABLESPOONS OF BUTTER in a non-stick frying pan over a medium to medium-high heat. Once the butter is completely melted and bubbly, add slices of egg-soaked challah to the pan. Once well browned, about 3 to 4 minutes, flip over. Brush honey over cooked side (using a pastry brush or the back of a spoon). Once the second side is crisp, flip all pieces so the honey-side makes contact with bottom of the pan for no more than 10 seconds. Flip the slices one last time, creating a nice caramelization on both sides. You want your french toast eggy and moist on the inside and brown and crispy on the outside.

TO ASSEMBLE, take two large plates and arrange with fresh fruit such as banana slices or strawberries. Place 1 slice of french toast on each plate, spoon half of the roasted apples on each slice, and then 2 slices of crispy ham. Gently lay the second piece of french toast on top of the ham, slightly askew from first piece. Top with more apples and remaining crispy ham slices. Using a small strainer gently shake confectioners' sugar over the entire dish.

Creative uses . . .

- You can use any type of several-days old bread, such as thick-cut white or wheat bread, brioche, or artisanal bread.

- I like to slice the cooked french toast into 1-inch sticks and keep them warm in the oven until the kids are ready for breakfast. Serve it to them with a small bowl of warm Nutella for dipping.

- Raisin bread is absolutely delicious with a drizzle of maple syrup.

SMOKED SALMON AND CHIVE
Scramble en Croissant

At the price of smoked salmon, you don't want to have to throw it away. Although you can use myriad ingredients for an egg scramble, this is one of the most decadent combinations. A simple topping here includes a dollop of crème fraîche and a generous sprinkle of Love Rub (page 29).

Serves 4

- 8 mini croissants
- 8 eggs
- 2 tablespoons chives, finely chopped
- 2 tablespoons Parmesan cheese, grated
- 2 tablespoons butter
- 1 tablespoon olive oil
- ¼ pound smoked salmon (about 4 slices), coarsely chopped
- 2 tablespoons crème fraîche
- 1 tablespoon *All-Purpose Love Rub* (page 29)
- 1 tomato, deseeded and diced (optional)

PREHEAT OVEN TO 400°F. Cut the top one-third off each croissant and carefully scoop out most of the dough from the bottom. Place tops and bottoms on a cookie sheet and put in oven for 3 to 5 minutes to crisp up the croissants.

WHISK TOGETHER EGGS, CHIVES, and cheese in a medium bowl. Heat the butter and oil in a non-stick pan over medium heat. Pour the egg mixture into the pan once the butter starts to bubble and then turn the heat to low. Stir with a wooden spoon, not allowing the eggs to brown. Once the eggs are almost set, fold in the smoked salmon and continue cooking until a small amount of liquid remains. You want to leave the eggs slightly runny and wet because they will continue cooking once you remove from the heat.

SPOON THE EGGS INTO THE CROISSANT bottom and finish with a dollop of crème fraîche, a sprinkle of *Love Rub,* and chopped tomatoes (optional). Replace the croissant top and serve.

Creative uses . . .
- *This recipe uses day-old croissants, but a small brioche bun or a sourdough roll would work just as well.*
- *You can top this dish off with my Everything Sauce (page 49), sour cream, or grated cheese.*

SUNNYSIDE EGGS
In Spicy Tomato Sauce

Have you ever seen someone order eggs for breakfast and then proceed to squeeze ketchup on them? This recipe is a refined way of combining eggs and fresh tangy tomato sauce and is a hearty and savory breakfast.

Serves 2

EGGS
3 cups *The Best Basic Tomato Sauce* (page 54)
4 eggs
1 tablespoon Parmesan cheese, grated

SOURDOUGH TOASTS
½ sourdough baguette
1 tablespoon olive oil
Salt and black pepper
1 garlic clove, peeled
1 teaspoon smoked paprika
1 tablespoon Parmesan cheese, grated

PREHEAT OVEN TO 400°F.

FOR SOURDOUGH TOASTS, cut the ends off the baguette and save one half for making croutons or breadcrumbs at another time. For the other half, slice the baguette into ½-inch slices on an angle. Lay slices on a baking sheet, drizzle a tablespoon of olive oil over the slices and sprinkle with salt and pepper. Bake for 3 to 5 minutes until lightly toasted. Take each individual toast and scrape the raw whole garlic very lightly on one side. Sprinkle paprika and freshly grated Parmesan over the garlic-scraped sides.

WARM THE TOMATO SAUCE in a medium-sized pan. Crack 2 eggs into a small bowl. With the back of a large spoon, make a small well in the sauce and slowly pour the eggs into the well. Repeat again with second set of 2 eggs. Sprinkle Parmesan (freshly grated if available) over the eggs and sauce, and cover. Cook until top of sunny side eggs begins to cloud over. Serve with sourdough toasts.

Creative uses . . .

- *If you don't have time to make fresh sauce and just happen to have half a jar of tomato sauce in your refrigerator, use the jar sauce in place of The Best Basic Tomato Sauce.*
- *Use any day old baguette if you don't have sourdough.*

BACON, ONION, AND OLIVE SOUFFLICHE

Just read the recipe title again and you will get why this is sooo delicious! I've named this a souffliche because it's eggy and creamy and has a bread crust like a quiche but it's also light and airy like a soufflé. This is a great way to use your leftover bread, the last few strips of bacon, the open jar of olives, and the last bit of hard cheese. I'm using black olives in this recipe but use any olives you have on hand. If your olives are in brine or a strong flavored liquid, rinse them before putting them in your souffliche.

Serves 4

5 slices day old bread, crusts removed, torn into 2-inch pieces
1 cup milk, heated
4 slices bacon, cut into crosswise strips
4 tablespoons butter
1 large onion, thinly sliced
2 sprigs fresh thyme (leaves only)
1 teaspoon anchovy paste (or 2 anchovies, finely chopped)
½ cup black olives, chopped
4 eggs, separated
¼ cup heavy cream
½ cup Parmesan cheese, grated
¼ cup hard cheese, grated (Gruyère, sharp cheddar)
2 teaspoons olive oil
Black pepper

PREHEAT OVEN TO 350°F Grease 4 (4-ounce) ramekins with butter.

POUR HEATED MILK over the bread pieces in a medium-sized bowl and soak for 5 minutes.

IN A NON-STICK PAN over a medium-high heat, cook the bacon until crispy. Remove bacon with slotted spoon and set aside. Place onions in the same pan and add butter, thyme, anchovy paste, and 2 teaspoons of oil. Cook over a low heat for 10 minutes, stirring frequently. Set aside to cool.

IN A SEPARATE BOWL, whisk egg yolks, cream, ¼ cup of the Parmesan, and the grated hard cheese. Add cooled onion mixture, bacon, olives, and soaked bread. Stir to combine.

WHISK THE EGG WHITES until they form stiff peaks. Fold them gently into the egg mixture. Pour equal amounts into ramekins and bake for 15 to 20 minutes. Once souffliches are golden brown in color and have puffed up over the top of the ramekins, take out of the oven and sprinkle each with remaining Parmesan, black pepper, and a drizzle of olive oil. Serve immediately.

Creative uses . . .

- *Turkey bacon or sausage works just as well as bacon. You can even dice up some leftover ham and cook until crispy.*

- *Add in leftover cooked vegetables in place of the olives and grate your favorite cheese into the mixture.*

- *Leave out the bacon, onions, and olive, and simply do a cheese souffliche. Delicious!*

HOMEMADE GRANOLA AND ORANGE ZEST
Vanilla Yogurt

I love granola but I don't like dry way-too-crunchy granola that feels like pebbles. This recipe has a good crunch and also a nice chewy texture. It's not too sweet and goes well with yogurt or by itself. Use any combination of mixed nuts and dried fruit that you have in your kitchen. This is a great way to use up excess dry goods in your pantry as well as creating a healthy snack for the family.

Makes 5 cups

GRANOLA

2 cups rolled oats
1 cup shredded coconut (sweetened or unsweetened)
¾ cup mixed nuts
½ cup flax seeds
1½ cups dried fruit (raisins, dried cranberries, apricots, or dates)
3 tablespoons brown sugar
½ teaspoon cinnamon
3 tablespoons honey
2 tablespoons agave syrup
1 teaspoon vanilla extract
¼ cup vegetable oil

ORANGE ZEST VANILLA YOGURT

2 (4-ounce) containers plain yogurt
1 orange, juiced and zested
1 teaspoon vanilla

GRANOLA

PREHEAT OVEN TO 275°F.
Place all dry ingredients in a large bowl. Mix together with your hands.

IN A SMALL BOWL, lightly whisk together the honey, agave syrup, vanilla, and oil. Once completely blended, pour over the dry mixture and using a plastic spatula, make sure the oats are thoroughly coated. Pour onto a baking sheet and spread out to a thin layer. Place in the oven for 1 hour, stirring and turning granola every fifteen minutes using your spatula. This is a crucial step to keep granola from burning.

TAKE OUT OF OVEN AND LET COOL. Break up large pieces and place in a sealable plastic bag. Serve with yogurt and *Mixed Fruit Coulis* (page 60).

ORANGE ZEST VANILLA YOGURT
Place a double layer of cheesecloth into a strainer and place in the sink. Pour yogurt into strainer and let drain for 40 minutes. Remove yogurt to a medium bowl. Add orange zest, juice of the orange, vanilla, and blend. Refrigerate for 1 hour before serving. Serve with fresh granola.

ROLLED CREPES STUFFED
with Mushrooms, Ricotta, and Prosciutto

CREPE BATTER
1 cup milk
1 egg
Salt
1½ cups flour
4 tablespoons butter

FILLING
2 tablespoons olive oil
1½ cup mushrooms,
    chopped
½ teaspoon each, salt and
    pepper
2 sprigs thyme (leaves only)
1 shallot, minced
8 ounces ricotta
4 slices prosciutto, cut into
    ½-inch strips

TOPPING
½ cup of *Gruyère, Cheddar,
    and Bleu Cheese Sauce*
    (page 52)
½ cup breadcrumbs or
    Homemade Breadcrumbs
    (page 19)
¼ cup Parmesan cheese,
    grated
1 teaspoon smoked paprika

PREHEAT OVEN TO 350°F.

CREPES
Make crepe batter by whisking together milk, egg, and a pinch of salt in a medium-sized bowl. Add half the flour and continue whisking. When just about incorporated, whisk the rest of the flour into the mixture. Add melted butter and whisk until smooth. Let rest for 30 minutes.

TO MAKE CREPES, begin with an 8 or 10-inch non-stick pan over medium heat. Once the pan is hot, wipe with butter and, using a 2-ounce ladle or tablespoon, pour batter into the center of the pan. Swirl the pan to create a thin layer of batter and cook for 2 minutes. Flip crepe and cook the second side for another minute. Remove to a plate and repeat for all 8 crepes.

FILLING
Take the same pan used for the crepes and add 1 tablespoon of olive oil. Once the oil is shimmering, add mushrooms to the pan and spread out in one layer. Drizzle another tablespoon of oil over them and do not stir or shake the pan. After 2 minutes, move the mushrooms around with a wooden spoon and add the shallots, thyme, salt, and pepper. Cook for 1 minute longer, stirring constantly.

STIR IN THE RICOTTA and remove from the heat. Fold in the prosciutto and set aside to cool.

FOR THE TOPPING, combine breadcrumbs with cheese and smoked paprika.

FILL EACH CREPE with about 2 heaping tablespoons of filling and roll up the crepes. Place the 8 crepes side by side in the baking dish and pour ½ cup of the cheese sauce over them. Top with seasoned breadcrumbs and bake for 30 minutes.

Creative uses . . .

- *Combine ricotta with leftover cooked vegetables for a quick delicious filling.*
- *Any leftover chicken, turkey, or ham will work for the filling. Try chopped cooked chicken, peas, and chopped chives.*
- *Try cooked spinach, ricotta, and a touch of crumbled bleu cheese. Goat cheese would also be a delicious addition.*
- *Use roasted tomatoes (page 54), basil, and toasted pine nuts and a spoonful of mascarpone.*
- *For a filling with a Mexican flavor, blend together sautéed onions and peppers, shredded cheese, beans, chopped parsley or cilantro, and two teaspoons of Chili Spice Blend (page 31).*
- *I love a sweet fruit filling in my breakfast crepes. In a medium bowl, mix together sliced overripe fruit, chopped dried fruit (optional), a teaspoon or two of brown sugar, and a squeeze of lemon. Fill the crepes with fruit mixture, sprinkle with cinnamon, and bake.*

Crepes are versatile because you can stuff them with so many delicious fillings. I created this recipe when I discovered a handful of mushrooms and an opened package of prosciutto in my fridge. I grabbed the half container of ricotta, a few eggs and an hour later I had a fabulous brunch.

Serves 4 (2 each)

CRISPY POTATO AND TURKEY SAUSAGE
Hash Browns

You can't have an egg breakfast without crispy, oniony potatoes. This dish is more like a potato and cheese tortilla from Spain than your traditional American hash brown. This is a great recipe to use up the potatoes on the counter or the leftover boiled or baked potatoes. When using a cooked potato, skip the additional 20 minutes of cook time with the onions. If the raw potatoes have "eyes," simply scoop them out. Don't worry about the look of the potato skin, you will be slicing and cooking them twice. They are best when cooked in a cast-iron skillet but any heavy bottomed pan will do.

Serves 4

2 potatoes
5 tablespoons olive oil
2 sprigs fresh rosemary, leaves only, or 1 teaspoon dried rosemary
2 turkey sausage links, taken out of the casing and crumbled
1 red onion, peeled and sliced thin
4 eggs
1 cup manchego cheese (or other hard cheese), grated
1 tablespoon *Savory Spice Blend (page 32)*
2 tablespoons flat-leaf parsley, chopped
1 teaspoon each of salt and black pepper

PREHEAT OVEN TO 400°F.

AFTER WASHING POTATOES, thinly slice the potatoes by first cutting them in half lengthwise and then ¼-inch slices from the short end. Place potato slices in a small clean towel and squeeze out all the excess water. Place in a large bowl.

IN A MEDIUM-SIZED FRYING PAN, heat 1 tablespoon of oil. Add rosemary to the pan for 30 seconds to infuse the oil with its fragrance. Add sausage and fry until golden brown and cooked through. Using a slotted spoon, remove the sausage and herbs from the pan and place on a paper towel to drain the excess oil.

ADD ANOTHER 2 TABLESPOONS OF OIL to the pan and cook potatoes and onions over high heat for 2 minutes. Lower the heat and continue cooking for 20 minutes, turning occasionally until potatoes are slightly golden.

COMBINE EGGS, CHEESE, SPICE BLEND, parsley, cooked sausage, salt, and black pepper in large bowl. Add the potatoes and mix gently until thoroughly coated.

WIPE OUT THE PAN with a sheet of paper towel, add the last 2 tablespoons of oil and place pan over low heat. Add the potato mixture and cook for 5 minutes. While cooking, use a spatula to lift the potatoes and allow the eggs to hit the bottom of the pan. Place pan on the top rack of your oven and cook for an additional 10 minutes until entire mixture is set and golden brown. Once the hash brown is taken out of the oven, run a sharp knife around the edge of the pan, place a large plate over the pan, and invert so potato hash brown comes out in one piece. Cut into wedges and garnish with a sprinkle of fresh chopped parsley.

VANILLA PANCAKES

1 cup buttermilk
1 cup ricotta cheese
2 eggs, separated
2 teaspoons vanilla extract
2 tablespoons sugar
½ cup cake flour
½ teaspoon baking powder
Pinch of salt
2 tablespoons butter (for greasing the griddle)
Confectioner's sugar (powdered sugar)

PLACE A GRIDDLE over two burners or use a large non-stick pan over medium high heat. In a large glass bowl, combine buttermilk, ricotta, egg yolks, and vanilla. Add sugar and gently whisk to dissolve. Sift the flour, baking powder, and salt into a separate bowl, then slowly add to wet mixture as you continue to whisk. Mix until thoroughly incorporated.

IN A SEPARATE BOWL, whisk or whip the 2 egg whites with a hand mixer until they turn from foamy to stiff peaks. Fold the egg whites into the batter by gently stirring from the bottom of the bowl with a soft plastic spatula.

USING A PAPER TOWEL to hold a small piece of butter, quickly rub the surface of the griddle or pan.

USING A SMALL LADLE (1 to 2-ounce) or a large spoon, pour the pancake batter into the same spot on the griddle until you have a nice round pancake. You want the grill hot enough that small bubbles begin to form on the tops of the pancakes. When the bottoms of the pancakes are golden brown, flip them over carefully and cook another 2 minutes. Total cooking time should not exceed 5 minutes. Serve warm with a dusting of confectioners' sugar.

These pancakes are light and creamy in the middle, unlike your more traditional cake-like pancake, and are a Sunday morning favorite at my house. Whenever I buy buttermilk, there is always half a quart left in the refrigerator. Other than baking, my top two uses for buttermilk are for fried chicken and pancakes. Don't let these pancakes sit for too long as they are best when eaten immediately.

Makes 12 to 14 (4-inch) pancakes.

CHAPTER 6: SMALL PLATES

Hors d'oeuvres and Appetizers

HOW MANY HORS D'OEUVRES?

Cooks find it difficult to plan how many hors d'oeuvres to prepare before a dinner and how many to prepare when the nibbles are the featured meal. I like to put hors d'oeuvres into two categories: one-bite and two-bites. There are some hors d' oeuvres that you pop in your mouth and slightly larger ones that you bite into at least once. To keep it simple, if you are serving a light to medium dinner after hors d'oeuvres, then consider serving six "bites" before the meal, which could be six to twelve pieces depending on the item. A skewered item (*Watermelon and Grape Tomato Skewers with Feta* page 90), is usually two to three bites, while a mini puff pastry hors d' oeuvre (*Goat Cheese and Melted Leeks en Croute with Raspberry Sauce* page 97) can be eaten in one to two bites. A typical two-hour cocktail party without dinner would require approximately ten bites, while a dinner-time event should provide closer to twenty bites since most people won't be having dinner afterward.

- Make sure to include vegetarian or vegan options for those who don't eat meat.

- A variety of hot and cold items will satisfy more people.

- A younger crowd tends to eat more than an older group of guests.

- Guests eat more at casual events than they do more formal events.

The easiest way to determine how many hors d'oeuvres to have and how many of each item to prepare, is to first identify what kind of event you are having. Longer parties where the hors d'oeuvres are the meal require more variety as well. Conversely, if the hors d'oeuvres precede a meal, you should offer fewer. I have provided a chart to give you a ballpark idea of how to plan and prepare for just about any occasion.

Every appetizer in this chapter benefits from using one or more salvage ingredients, thereby reducing the cost and making home entertaining more affordable. Many appetizers can be made ahead of time and reheated when your guests begin to arrive.

Event	Total number of guests	Number of items to prepare	Number of pieces per person	Number of pieces per item	Total number of pieces
2-HOUR PARTY (hors d'oeuvres only)	Up to 20	4	10	50	200
	20 to 40	5	10	60	300
	40 to 60	8	10	70 to 80	500
	60+	9 to 10	10	75 to 80	750
2-HOUR PARTY (dinner time*)	Up to 20	4	20	100	400
	20 to 40	5	20	120	600
	40 to 60	8	20	140 to 160	1,000
	60+	9 to 10	20	150 to 175	1,500
PARTY FOLLOWED BY 2 TO 3 COURSE MEAL**	Up to 20	4	6	30	120
	20 to 40	5	6	40	200
	40 to 60	8	6	60	300
	60+	8	6	60 to 75	450

*When serving hors d'oeuvres between 6 p.m. and 9 p.m., try to include a substantial dinner-type item such as *Mini Sea Bass Wellington with Roasted Asparagus and Dill Crème Fraîche* (page 100). Also include a dessert item like *Strawberry Cheesecake Bars* (page 254).

**If serving hors d'oeuvres before a 4-course meal, decrease the number of items by 50 percent.

WATERMELON AND GRAPE TOMATO
Skewers with Feta

Not only do these skewers look scrumptious and colorful, they are refreshing and satisfying. This is the perfect nibble to complement meat or chicken hors d'oeuvres when serving more than one item.

Serves 2 (6 skewers)

½ pint grape tomatoes, sliced in half
1 teaspoon salt
1 cup watermelon, cut into 1-inch cubes
1 tablespoon olive oil
¼ cup feta, crumbled
6 (6-inch) wooden skewers

PLACE TOMATOES IN A SMALL BOWL and toss with salt. Let the tomatoes sit for 20 to 30 minutes to bring out the natural flavors.

STARTING WITH A TOMATO HALF, alternate with watermelon pieces by piercing fruit in the middle and sliding down the skewer. Leave about ½ inch on each end. Finish with a tomato half. Lay skewers on a platter, drizzle with olive oil, and sprinkle generously with feta cheese.

Creative uses . . .
- *Cherry tomatoes work well as do other fruits such as grapes. Goat cheese works well if you have it.*
- *For a more exotic skewer, try kiwi, pineapple, and mango with a sprinkle of dried coconut in place of cheese.*

CRISPY FRIED OLIVES, ARTICHOKE HEARTS,
and Bacon Truffle Tater Tots

A simple breading technique transforms these refrigerator staples into scrumptious snacks or a crispy appetizer when served together. Any pitted olive will do as long as you rinse them prior to breading. I like to soak them in buttermilk overnight to eliminate the briny flavor. You can use any soft cheese to stuff your olives, or fry them without cheese.

Serves 4

4 ounces pitted olives (about 14–16 olives), drained and rinsed
1 cup buttermilk
4 ounces artichoke hearts, drained and rinsed
8 ounces mashed potatoes
2 strips bacon, cut into crosswise strips
1 teaspoon truffle oil (optional)
2 tablespoons *All-Purpose Love Rub* (page 29)

BREADING STATION

1 cup flour
2 eggs
1 teaspoon chili paste (or spicy mustard)
1 cup breadcrumbs
2 teaspoons *All-Purpose Love Rub* (page 29)
Salt
4 cups vegetable oil

AFTER RINSING OLIVES, place in a resealable plastic bag with buttermilk. Seal and place in the refrigerator for an hour before breading. You can soak them overnight if you have the time. This removes all the salt and the acidity of the buttermilk softens the olive as well. Dry the olives and artichoke hearts with a paper towel.

ADD BACON TO A MEDIUM-SIZED PAN and place over a medium heat. Cook bacon until crispy and remove to a paper towel to drain excess oil. Combine mashed potatoes, bacon, truffle oil, and spice blend. With wet hands, take a heaping tablespoon of potato mixture and shape into a short thick cylinder (like a tater tot). Repeat with remaining potatoes.

SET UP YOUR BREADING STATION with three shallow bowls. Place flour in the first bowl, the eggs and chili paste in the second bowl, and breadcrumbs with spice blend in the third. Add a generous pinch of salt to all three bowls and mix until the ingredients in all bowls are well combined.

GENTLY ROLL OLIVES, ARTICHOKES, AND TATER TOTS in the seasoned flour and shake off any excess. Next, place them in the egg mixture then into the bread-crumbs. Make sure all items are completely covered with breadcrumbs and place on a platter. When you are finished breading all the items, place the platter in the refrigerator for an hour so the breading can set. *This is an important step to avoid your breading from coming off in the oil.*

HEAT OIL IN A MEDIUM POT until a deep frying ther-mometer reaches between 350° and 375°F. If you don't have a thermometer, place a small cube of bread into the oil. If the bread browns in 60 seconds, the temperature is approximately 360°F.

FRY IN SMALL BATCHES without overcrowding the pot. When the olives and artichokes float to the top, remove them from the oil with a slotted spoon and place on a paper towel. Immediately sprinkle with spice blend. Potatoes will need another 2 minutes. Serve with tartar sauce or *Chili Mayo* (page 104).

FRESH SHRIMP POACHED
in Olive Oil and Garlic

One of my favorite ways to cook shrimp is to poach them so they don't overcook. The oil, flavored with pungent garlic and fiery chiles in this dish, gives you tender shrimp that are perfect for part of a tapas spread or as an appetizer.

Serves 6

1 pound medium (16 to 20 per pound) raw shrimp
½ cup olive oil
¼ teaspoon crushed red pepper flakes
1 lemon, halved
2 garlic cloves, thinly sliced
¼ cup chopped fresh parsley
1 teaspoon smoked Spanish paprika (*pimentón de la vera*)
Salt and black pepper to taste

PEEL AND DEVEIN SHRIMP leaving tails attached. Rinse shrimp and pat dry on paper towels.

COMBINE OIL, CRUSHED RED PEPPER FLAKES, lemon (cut-side down), and garlic in a small saucepan. Cook over low heat for 8 minutes or until garlic is golden brown. Be careful not to burn the garlic. Add shrimp, stir to coat, and take the pan off the heat. Cover the pan and allow shrimp to poach for 10 minutes.

TRANSFER SHRIMP TO A PLATTER and spoon crispy garlic and olive oil over them. To serve, squeeze lemon from oil over shrimp and sprinkle with parsley, paprika, salt, and pepper. Serve hot or at room temperature.

The shrimp can be prepared up to two days in advance and refrigerated, tightly covered. Reheat them in the olive oil prior to serving.

GOAT CHEESE AND MELTED LEEKS
en Croute with Raspberry Sauce

This delicious one-bite appetizer can be prepared with any type of onion you have on hand. When I have a few scallions or a leftover leek in my refrigerator, I love to make this hors d'oeuvre. I prefer a strong goat cheese but you can use brie, bleu, or any soft cheese. The sweet raspberry sauce is optional but is a wonderful compliment to the saltiness of the cheese. Use any berries you have on hand.

Serves 4

SAUCE (optional)
½ cup raspberries
2 tablespoons granulated
    sugar
2 tablespoons water

PASTRY
1 sheet (12 by 16-inch) puff
    pastry
Flour for rolling out the
    pastry
1 tablespoon olive oil
1 leek, onion, or 3 scallions,
    roughly chopped
Salt
2 ounces goat cheese
1 egg, beaten

PREHEAT OVEN TO 350°F.

COMBINE BERRIES, SUGAR, AND WATER in a small pot and bring to a boil. Continue boiling for 5 minutes, then take off heat to cool. Purée in a blender or food processor and strain to remove seeds.

PLACE A SMALL PAN OVER MEDIUM HEAT and add oil, leeks, and a pinch of salt. Shake the pan to coat the leeks and keep them from burning. (Use the same procedure if using an onion or scallion). Turn the heat to low and continue cooking until leeks are wilted and beginning to brown, about 3 minutes. Set aside to cool.

ON A WELL-FLOURED SURFACE, roll out the puff pastry to ¼ inch. Using a sharp knife, cut dough into 12 equal squares. Place a small pinch of leeks in the center of each square. Place a small piece of cheese (about the size of 1 teaspoon) on top of the leeks. Fold the corner closest to you over the cheese and then fold the two "wings" on either side toward the middle as you roll the pastry forward. You want to end up with the leeks on top. Cut away any excess dough. Repeat with the remaining squares and place them on a lightly greased cookie sheet.

USING A PASTRY BRUSH, lightly coat the surface of each pastry with egg wash and place in the oven for 8 minutes, or until pastry is golden in color and puffed. Serve warm with raspberry sauce.

Creative uses . . .
- *Puff pastry is so versatile and can transform many of your leftover ingredients into delicious appetizers. Try chopped cooked vegetables with a sprinkle of Parmesan cheese.*
- *A delicious salty hors d'oeuvre combines cream cheese and smoked salmon in the puff pastry.*
- *Also delicious in puff pastry are dried fruits, such as dates, complemented with bleu cheese.*

HOW TO CLEAN LEEKS

Cut off the root end and approximately 2 inches of the green end, then slice the leek in half, lengthwise. Slice the leek halves into ½-inch crosswise strips and place in a bowl of cold water. Give the leek pieces a stir with your fingers and then carefully remove the pieces that have floated to the top. Be careful to allow the dirt to settle to the bottom of the bowl as you scoop up the clean pieces of leek. Dry the leeks in a paper towel before using. Can be done ahead of time and kept in the freezer in a resealable bag.

MINI SEA BASS WELLINGTON WITH ROASTED ASPARAGUS
and Dill Crème Fraîche

1 sheet (12 by 16-inch) puff pastry
Flour for rolling out the pastry
½ cup crème fraîche (or sour cream)
2 teaspoons of fresh dill, finely chopped
8 ounces of sea bass, cooked
3 asparagus spears, roughly chopped
Olive oil
Salt
1 egg, beaten

PREHEAT OVEN TO 350°F.

GENTLY SAUTÉ the asparagus in a pan with olive oil until they begin to brown. Remove to cool.

COMBINE CRÈME FRAÎCHE AND FRESH DILL in a small bowl. If crème fraîche is too stiff, add a squeeze of lemon. Keep refrigerated until use.

ON A WELL-FLOURED SURFACE, roll out the puff pastry to ¼ inch. Using a sharp knife, cut dough into 8 equal squares. Place a teaspoon of asparagus in the center of each square. Place 1 ounce of sea bass (about a 1½ to 2-inch piece) on top of the asparagus. Fold the corner closest to you over the fish and then fold the two "wings" on either side towards the middle as you roll the pastry forward. You want to end up with the asparagus on top. Cut away any excess dough. Repeat with the remaining squares and place them on a lightly greased cookie sheet.

USING A PASTRY BRUSH, lightly coat the surface of each pastry with egg wash and place in the oven for 8 minutes or until pastry is golden in color and puffed. Serve warm with crème fraîche.

Creative uses . . .

- *Try any white flaky fish like tilapia or flounder instead of sea bass and combine with fresh cut or roasted tomatoes (page 54). The tomatoes will soften and sweeten naturally as the puff pastry cooks, and the fish will be cooked perfectly.*
- *Use leftover cooked meat or chicken instead of fish. Combine with vegetables and fresh herbs you have on hand.*

Leftover fish is one of the most difficult things for most cooks to deal with. Reheating fish usually results in a dry rubbery texture. After "pigs in a blanket," my favorite puff pastry appetizer is fish with a roasted vegetable, dipped in crème fraîche with herbs. This version uses leftover sea bass and a few spears of asparagus that didn't make it to the steamer. Some fresh dill and a sheet of puff pastry out of the freezer, and you'll have a rich and delicious hors d'oeuvre. Sour cream works if you don't have crème fraîche or you can squeeze half a lemon into 8 ounces of cream cheese and whip until smooth.

Serves 4

FLAT IRON STEAK "SUSHI ROLL"
with Spicy Scrambled Eggs and Smoked Salmon

My version of steak and eggs begins with a perfectly cooked leftover NY strip (or any leftover steak), sliced thin and wrapped around well-seasoned scrambled eggs. The addition of smoked salmon and trout caviar is a special treat that gives the final plate elegance if you have the ingredients on hand.

Serves 4

12 ounces cooked steak (8 slices), room temperature, sliced on the bias to about ¼-inch thickness
2 eggs
½ tablespoon butter
½ teaspoon Sriracha or chili paste (optional)
½ cup crème fraîche
1 teaspoon *All-Purpose Love Rub* (page 29)
4 ounces of smoked salmon, cut into ½-inch wide strips
1 ounce smoked caviar
1 tablespoon chives, finely chopped
Salt and black pepper

MELT THE BUTTER in a non-stick pan. Lightly beat the eggs and Sriracha and pour into the pan. Scramble until light and fluffy. Add a pinch of salt and some black pepper to taste.

MIX CRÈME FRAÎCHE with spice blend until combined.

ROLL STEAK SLICE around a small spoonful of eggs and place on a platter with eggs facing upward. Wrap each steak and egg bundle in a strip of smoked salmon, top with a small dollop of crème fraîche, ¼ teaspoon of caviar, and a sprinkle of chives.

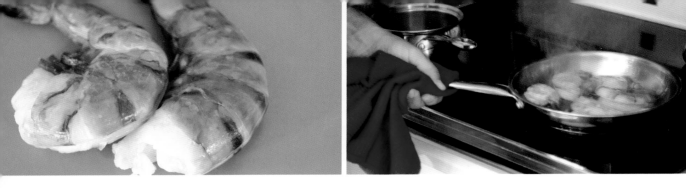

PROSCIUTTO-WRAPPED SHRIMP
with Avocado and Mango

Many households across the country have these or similar ingredients on hand to work with: leftover cooked shrimp, ham or prosciutto (or bacon works well), a ripe avocado, a mango (or papaya or kiwi), and any large leaf lettuce. This recipe is all about flavor and texture combinations. You have the cool lettuce, the crispy prosciutto, tender shrimp, creamy avocado, sweet mango, and the perfectly spiced chili mayo to tie it all together. If you don't have shrimp on hand, you can substitute scallops and even chunks of cooked fish.

CHILI MAYO
½ cup mayonnaise
1 tablespoon *All-Purpose Love Rub* (page 29)
½ lemon, juiced
1 teaspoon olive oil

SHRIMP
8 large cooked shrimp (or see below for cooking method)
4 slices prosciutto, cut in half lengthwise
8 lettuce leaves
1 avocado, cut in half, removed from skin, and cut into ½-inch slices
1 mango, cut into ½-inch slices

PREHEAT OVEN TO BROIL.
Rinse and pat dry 8 lettuce cups and refrigerate until ready to serve. Squeeze fresh lemon juice over sliced avocado.

CHILI MAYO
Combine mayonnaise, spice blend, lemon juice, and olive oil. Season with salt and black pepper.

WRAP THE PROSCUITTO around each shrimp so it overlaps by about ½ inch and stick with a toothpick to hold in place. Place wrapped shrimp on a baking sheet and place on top rack of oven. Broil for 2 minutes and then turn the shrimp for another 2 minutes or until prosciutto is slightly brown and crispy.

TO SERVE, smear mayo on the inside of the lettuce cup, add a shrimp and a slice of avocado and mango.

If using raw shrimp, season the shrimp well with salt and black pepper and preheat oven to 400°F. After wrapping the shrimp with prosciutto, place in the oven for 6 to 8 minutes on the first side and an additional 3 minutes on the second side until the prosciutto is crispy and the shrimp is cooked through.

Serves 4

ROASTED RED PEPPER "SUSHI ROLL"
Stuffed with Italian Sausage

Once opened, a jar of roasted red peppers can get moldy within a week. Although there are several methods of extending the shelf life of these delicious tender peppers (see below), I like to transform them into sushi-like rolls. You can stuff them with leftover hamburger, ground turkey, beef, or sausage, chop them up in a salad or omelet, blend them into a sauce, or eat them with a piece of crusty bread, roasted garlic, and olive oil. These stuffed pepper rolls can be made ahead of time and roasted right before serving.

Serves 4

4 roasted red peppers, sliced into 2-inch wide strips (about 3 to 4 inches long)
¼ pound cooked ground sausage or leftover hamburger or ground beef
1 tablespoon ricotta (or mascarpone)
Red chili flakes

PREHEAT OVEN TO 350°F.

COMBINE GROUND MEAT, RICOTTA, and a sprinkle of red chili flakes. With wet hands, form small balls (about 1 tablespoon) and place on the inside of each pepper strip. Carefully roll the pepper until there is a slight overlap (about ½ inch), and secure with a toothpick.

PLACE THE ROLLS ON A BAKING SHEET so that ground meat is facing upward, and bake for 10 minutes until the edges of the peppers begin to char. Remove toothpicks and serve.

STORING ROASTED RED PEPPERS

Once you open a jar of roasted red peppers, depending on the brand, the acidity level of the solution, and the temperature of your refrigerator, the shelf life can range between several days and two weeks. To keep roasted red peppers after opening (as well as artichoke hearts and olives), fill the jar to the top with olive oil. You can also add vinegar, a natural bacteria inhibitor, to the jar. Freezing roasted red peppers (between small sheets of wax paper) works as well, and they will last in the freezer for six months with only a slight change in the texture.

Photo credit: ThinkStock

BRUSCHETTA WITH GOAT CHEESE
and Sun-dried Tomatoes

I made this more than twenty years ago for my mother and her friends at her summer house in Montauk, and they named it Love Bread. This could possibly be my favorite bread appetizer and is further proof that bruschetta should be its own food group. Use roasted tomatoes or roasted red peppers in place of or in addition to sun-dried tomatoes. Any spreadable cheese will work here and, as always, lead with your favorite fresh herbs or combination of dry herbs.

Serves 8 (2 pieces per person)

1 loaf crusty bread (preferably a baguette)

4 tablespoons olive oil

1 teaspoon red chili flakes

1 tablespoon fresh thyme (leaves only), finely chopped, or 1 teaspoon dried thyme

1 tablespoon fresh rosemary (leaves only), finely chopped, or 1 teaspoon dried rosemary

1 tablespoon parsley, finely chopped

1 tablespoon capers, drained and chopped

4 ounces goat cheese, softened

½ cup sun-dried tomatoes in oil, drained and chopped

¼ cup Parmesan cheese, grated

PREHEAT OVEN TO 375°F.

SLICE BAGUETTE IN HALF horizontally and place both halves cut side up in the oven (directly on rack) for 3 minutes, just enough to lightly toast it.

PLACE A SMALL PAN on a medium heat and add 4 tablespoons of olive oil. Add the chili flake, chopped herbs, and capers and cook on medium heat for 5 minutes to toast the herbs.

WHEN THE BREAD IS SLIGHTLY TOASTED, remove from the oven and spread the goat cheese on both halves. Sprinkle the chopped sun-dried tomatoes over the goat cheese and put back in the oven for 2 to 3 minutes to soften the cheese and slightly char the tomatoes.

REMOVE FROM THE OVEN and pour the herbs in oil mixture evenly over the bread. Finish with a generous amount of freshly grated Parmesan, cut into wedges, and serve.

ASPARAGUS RICOTTA BRUSCHETTA
with Crispy Fried Shallots

My mother loves asparagus, and on any given week will have 4 to 6 spears in her refrigerator leftover from dinner. You can substitute broccoli, green beans, cauliflower, peas, or beans to make this topping. In Italy, bruschetta is traditionally a garlic-rubbed toast, topped with olive oil, vegetables, meats, and just about anything. This version contrasts a smooth creamy asparagus purée with crunchy sliced shallots as the topping. Red or white onions can be substituted for the shallots.

Serves 4

4 cups vegetable oil
1 cup flour
1 teaspoon salt
1 teaspoon smoked paprika
1 shallot, peeled and sliced thin into small rings
½ pound fresh asparagus
½ cup ricotta cheese
2 to 3 sprigs fresh thyme (leaves only)
1½ teaspoon salt
½ teaspoon black pepper
4 tablespoon olive oil
1 baguette, sliced horizontally
1 garlic clove, peeled and whole

PREHEAT OVEN TO 400°F.

HEAT VEGETABLE OIL IN A MEDIUM POT until a deep frying thermometer reaches between 350° and 375°F. If you don't have a thermometer, place a small cube of bread into the oil. If the bread browns in 60 seconds, the temperature is approximately 360°F.

COMBINE THE FLOUR, 1 teaspoon salt, and 1 teaspoon smoked paprika in a small bowl. Add sliced shallots to the bowl and coat completely with flour. Drop in the hot oil and fry for 1 minute until slightly golden and crispy. Using your deep-frying scoop, remove the shallots to a paper towel-lined plate, sprinkle with salt, and set aside. If you are making more bruschetta, you will need to fry the shallots in batches.

FILL A MEDIUM POT about two-thirds with water and bring to a boil. Add 1 tablespoon of salt and drop in the asparagus. After 60 seconds, take pot off the heat and drain. Place asparagus in a bowl of salted ice water (ice bath). This will stop the cooking process and keep your asparagus bright green and crunchy. After a few minutes, drain and transfer to a mini food processor. Add ricotta, thyme, salt, pepper, and 1 tablespoon of olive oil. Purée for 10 seconds until smooth. Set aside.

PLACE BAGUETTE HALVES on a baking sheet, drizzle with 1 tablespoon of oil and place in the oven for 4 to 5 minutes until light brown and crispy. Remove from oven and let cool. Gently scrape the whole garlic on one side. This will impart a lot of garlic flavor, so don't overdo it.

SPREAD A GENEROUS LAYER of vegetable/ricotta mixture on both baguette halves, then top with fried shallots. Sprinkle with black pepper and drizzle with a tablespoon of oil. Cut into slices and serve immediately.

SEARED SCALLOP ON TOAST
with Avocado, Cucumber, Tomato, and Mango Salsa

Although this is one of the more elegant looking dishes, the ingredients are simple, and I usually have them available. The salsa can be altered to suit your taste or to what you have in your refrigerator. Substitutions can include pineapple for the mango and a simple salsa of tomato and cucumber. This dish also works with shrimp as well as any fish you may have on hand, either fresh or previously cooked. The toast is more of a "handle" and something to soak up the salsa juices than an integral part of the dish, so you can serve the scallops with just the salsa or make them part of a salad.

Serves 4

SALSA

½ avocado, diced
½ cucumber, diced
1 tomato, cut in half,
   pulp scooped out and
   discarded, diced
½ mango, diced
1 lime, zested and juiced
1 tablespoon cilantro, finely
   chopped (optional)
1 teaspoon *Savory Spice
   Blend* (page 32)

SCALLOPS

8 sea scallops
1 tablespoon olive oil
Salt
Pinch of *Savory Spice Blend*
4 slices of wheat bread,
   crusts removed, cut in half
   diagonally

COMBINE ALL INGREDIENTS FOR SALSA in a glass bowl and refrigerate.

HEAT 1 TABLESPOON OF OIL in a non-stick pan over medium high heat. Sprinkle salt on both sides of each scallop and place in hot pan. Cook for 3 minutes and turn to sear the other side for 2 minutes.

TOAST THE BREAD UNDER THE BROILER for 1 to 2 minutes or in a toaster oven. Place a scallop in the center of each toast triangle and top with salsa. Sprinkle with spice blend and serve.

CHAPTER 7: THE BOUNTIFUL BOWL

Mmm ... mmm ... Soup!

Everyone who knows me knows I love making soup. Soups are a great way of using leftovers as well as vegetables that have passed their peak of freshness. Epicure Gourmet Market & Café has been making homemade soups for more than forty years and I am fortunate to have had the opportunity to create a new line of all-natural soups for them. Most soups start with a basic beginning of carrot, celery, onion (or leek), and garlic, all of which are rough chopped and then softened over a medium heat. A main ingredient and stock (or water) is added, and then the most important ingredient, *time*, works its magic. Basic soups and stocks can be made in as little as 10 minutes or can simmer for hours as they develop flavor and complexity. The soups in this chapter (some of them from the Epicure with Love line) range from clear broths to purées to chunkier soups and different types of chili. They can be prepared with leftover items in your refrigerator, unused ingredients that are past their prime, fresh ingredients, or in combination with each other.

SOUP MAKING TIPS

1. TAKE STOCK—Most chefs will tell you the quality of your stock will determine the quality of your soup. Although you can use water, bouillon cubes, or canned stocks, homemade stock (pages 117–119) is always best and can take as little as 10 to 20 minutes. Stock also freezes well so you can store plenty in your freezer.
2. SOUP PARTNER—Soups can be enhanced with the addition of one or more ingredients from your kitchen. A swirl of yogurt, heavy cream, sour cream, or crème fraîche gives soup a velvety texture and lightens the color. A drizzle of olive oil or infused oils can give the soup another layer of flavor and richness. The addition of grated Parmesan cheese, a spoonful of goat cheese, or a crumble of bleu or feta cheese can be the perfect finisher. Crusty bread is the best partner for your homemade soup, but you can also add a tasty crunch by adding homemade croutons (page 19).
3. REHEATING—Gently and slowly reheat your soup. Never let your soup come to a boil as it can scorch the soup and alter the flavor.
4. THICKEN OR THIN—Although most soups taste better the next day, they can thicken as well. Slowly reheat with the addition of a little water (about ¼ to ½ cup) or some stock. If you find your soup is too watery or thin, add a spoonful of cooked mashed potatoes or canned beans while heating. During soup making, you can add some diced potatoes, which will release their starch and cause the soup to naturally thicken.

ALL-NATURAL VEGETABLE BROTH

When I created the Epicure with Love line of soups, I decided to use a vegetable stock as my base. As with most stocks, it begins with carrot, celery, onion, leeks, and garlic, but also includes some fresh herbs and dried spices for depth. This stock is amazing for all soups, perfect for simmering vegetables, and is delicious as a broth.

Makes 3 quarts

- 2 medium onions, roughly chopped
- 1 leek, roughly chopped
- 2 garlic cloves, minced
- 3 celery stalks, roughly chopped
- 1 turnip, quartered
- 2 carrots, peeled and roughly chopped
- ½ tomato, roughly chopped
- 1 small bunch fresh parsley
- 1 small bunch fresh cilantro
- 3 bay leaves
- 2 cloves
- 8 black peppercorns

ADD LEEKS AND ONIONS (small amount of butter or oil is optional) to a stock pot over medium heat and cook until soft and fragrant, about 8 minutes. Stir frequently to keep vegetables from burning. Add garlic for 2 to 3 more minutes until sharp fragrance of garlic softens. Add celery, turnip, and carrot, and cook for another 5 minutes. Continue stirring to keep vegetables from browning.

ADD WATER AND TOMATO AND BRING TO A BOIL. Skim any impurities that come to the surface. Reduce heat and simmer for 40 minutes. Add herbs and spices and simmer for an additional 15 minutes. Remove from heat, allow to cool, then strain.

HOMEMADE CHICKEN SOUP
with Dill

Chicken soup is delicious, warming, comforting, healing, and healthy. My mother's soup was made from fresh chicken stock, had a hint of citrus, and was loaded with parsley and dill. This is the ultimate salvage soup for leftovers or left behind produce. You can use store-bought chicken stock to make this soup, but I always prefer homemade stock. Use my All-Natural Vegetable Stock (page 117) *or my* Chicken Stock (below).

Serves 8

CHICKEN STOCK
1 whole chicken (about 3 pounds)
2 carrots, peeled and rough chopped
2 celery stalks, rough chopped
1 turnip, unpeeled and halved
3 medium onions, unpeeled and halved
1 garlic head, cut in half crosswise
2 bay leaves
3 fresh sage leaves
4 sprigs fresh thyme
8 sprigs fresh parsley
2 teaspoons salt
10 whole peppercorns
½ lemon

STOCK

AFTER THOROUGHLY WASHING THE CHICKEN (inside and out), place in a large soup pot and add all the vegetables, herbs, peppercorns, and salt. Add enough cold water to completely cover the chicken (about 3 quarts) and bring to a boil. Use either a mesh skimmer or large spoon to skim off the grayish foam that rises to the top. When the pot comes to a boil, immediately turn down the temperature to low and simmer uncovered for 45 minutes.

REMOVE THE CHICKEN from the soup pot and set aside to cool as the stock continues to simmer. Once cooled, remove the meat from the bones and return the carcass to the soup pot. Reserve meat for chicken salad (page 144) or chicken soup (page 120). Add lemon half and continue simmering for 2 more hours.

REMOVE THE CARCASS and strain the stock into 1-quart containers and refrigerate uncovered. Once the stock solidifies in the refrigerator (about 2 hours), skim the fat that has risen to the surface. Continue with soup recipe or place sealable lids on the containers and move to the freezer for storage.

CHICKEN SOUP

2 tablespoons olive oil
4 sprigs fresh thyme
1 sprig fresh rosemary
1 large onion, peeled and
　rough chopped
2 garlic cloves, minced
2 carrots, peeled and cut
　on an angle into ½-inch
　pieces
3 celery stalks, chopped into
　½-inch pieces
1 bay leaf
2 quarts chicken stock (see
　119)
4 sprigs fresh dill
6 sprigs fresh parsley
2 cups cooked chicken (from
　stock making or leftover)
Salt and black pepper

SOUP

IN A LARGE SOUP POT or Dutch oven, heat 2 tablespoons of oil over medium heat. Add thyme and rosemary and stir for 2 minutes to infuse the oil with the herbs' flavors. Add onions and stir to thoroughly coat the onions with the herbs and oil. Cook for 5 minutes to soften. Add garlic, stir, and cook for an additional 2 minutes. Be careful not to brown the onions or the garlic.

ADD THE CARROTS AND CELERY and cook another 6 to 8 minutes to soften the vegetables, stirring frequently. Add bay leaf, stock, 1 teaspoon of salt, and ½ teaspoon of black pepper. Bring to a boil then lower the heat and simmer for 1 hour. Stir in dill and parsley. Season to taste.

ADD COOKED CHICKEN and simmer for another 2 minutes to warm through. Pour into soup bowls and garnish with a fresh sprig of dill.

8 VEGETABLE PURÉE SOUP

This is one of the bestselling soups at Epicure, and one of the healthiest. The curry and onion powders are perfect partners for these hearty root vegetables. Don't worry if you don't have all the ingredients. Use what you have.

Makes 3 to 4 quarts

2 tablespoons butter
2 onions, peeled and rough chopped
1 leek, sliced lengthwise and then into ½-inch strips
1 tablespoon garlic, minced
3 carrots, peeled and rough chopped
2 celery stalks, rough chopped
½ head cauliflower, cut into 1-inch chunks
1 turnip, peeled and cut in half
1½ cups white wine
3 quarts *All Natural Vegetable Stock* (page 117), plus 1 cup for blending spices
1 cup milk
3 potatoes, peeled and diced
2 teaspoons onion powder
2 teaspoons curry powder
Salt
¼ cup plain yogurt (optional)
Chili oil (optional)

IN A LARGE SOUP POT, melt butter over medium heat and add onions and leeks. Cook until softened and fragrant, about 8 minutes. Then add garlic for another 2 minutes until fragrance softens. Add remaining vegetables (except potatoes). Continue cooking until vegetables soften, about 6 minutes.

ADD WINE TO DEGLAZE THE POT. Using a wooden spoon, scrap the bottom of the pot and loosen any vegetable pieces that have stuck to the bottom. Lower the heat to a simmer and cook until liquid is reduced by half, about 8 to 10 minutes.

ADD VEGETABLE STOCK and bring to a boil. Skim any impurities that come to the surface. Reduce heat and simmer for 25 minutes. Add milk and potatoes. Simmer another 15 minutes until potatoes are tender. Once potatoes are fork tender, remove from heat.

USING AN IMMERSION BLENDER, purée the mixture until smooth. You can also purée in batches using a traditional blender.

WHISK CURRY POWDER and onion powder in a bowl with 1 cup of warm vegetable stock. Add to soup and taste for seasoning. Serve with a dollop of yogurt and a drizzle of olive oil.

ROASTED TOMATO
and Basil Soup

2 pounds tomatoes, cut in half
1 tablespoon of salt
3 tablespoons olive oil
½ red onion, quartered (leave the skin on)
1 white or yellow onion, peeled and rough chopped
4 garlic cloves, peeled and smashed
1 jalapeño, halved (remove seeds if you want less heat)
1 small handful of parsley
3 to 4 sprigs fresh thyme

1 sprig fresh rosemary
1 (14-ounce) can whole tomatoes
2 cups *All-Natural Vegetable Stock* (page 117) or *Chicken Stock* (page 119)
2 bay leaves
4 to 5 fresh basil leaves, finely chopped
½ cup heavy cream
2 tablespoon butter
1 tablespoon smoked paprika
Salt and ground pepper

PREHEAT OVEN TO 400°F.
Place a large roasting pan in the hot oven for 10 minutes while you prep the vegetables. Place tomatoes in a bowl and sprinkle generously with salt. Set aside for 10 to 15 minutes.

CAREFULLY REMOVE THE ROASTING PAN from the oven and add 2 tablespoons of oil, onions, garlic, jalapeño, and herbs. Stir the vegetables to combine as they sizzle and return to oven. Roast for 10 minutes until onions begin to brown.

ADD FRESH AND CANNED TOMATOES to the roasting pan and drizzle with remaining tablespoon of oil and a generous pinch of salt. Mix well, return to oven, and continue roasting until tomatoes begin to char, about 20 minutes.

TRANSFER TO A MEDIUM POT and add stock, bay leaves, and bring to a boil. Lower the heat, stir in half the basil, and simmer for another 20 minutes, skimming the surface of any foam.

USE TONGS TO REMOVE HERB STEMS and bay leaves and discard. Allow soup to cool (about 10 minutes), stir in remaining basil, and blend until smooth with an immersion blender.

YOU can use a regular blender but you will have to blend the soup in batches.

RETURN BLENDED SOUP TO POT over a medium-high heat. Once soup is at a simmer, add cream. Continue simmering for 5 minutes and then stir in butter and smoked paprika. Taste for seasoning. Add salt and black pepper if needed. Ladle into soup bowls, garnish with basil leaf.

SERVE with fresh croutons (page 19), garlic bread, or a grilled cheese sandwich (page 140).

This rich and flavorful classic can be made in under an hour. I love using a variety of tomatoes and onions depending on what I have. The flavor imparted from roasting is deep and smoky and brings out the natural flavors of the tomatoes but you can absolutely make this soup on the stovetop by simmering the vegetables from the start. I always keep a batch of roasted tomatoes (page 54) in the freezer, which you can toss in the pot with the canned tomatoes.

 To cut the calories, use milk instead of cream and leave out the butter.

 Makes 1 to 1½ quarts

ASPARAGUS VICHYSSOISE

Makes 2 quarts

2 to 2½ pounds asparagus,
  stalks cut into 1-inch
  pieces, reserve tips
2 to 3 sprigs fresh thyme
1 quart, plus 1 cup *All-
  Natural Vegetable Stock*
  (page 117)
2 tablespoons butter
2 leeks, cleaned and cut into
  ½-inch slices (page 99)
1 bay leaf
½ pound potatoes
8 ounces milk
2 teaspoons salt
¼ teaspoon white pepper

IN A LARGE POT, ADD ASPARAGUS STALKS, thyme, vegetable stock, and 2 cups of water. Bring to a boil and simmer for 20 minutes to infuse asparagus flavor. Strain and keep warm.

USING A FOOD PROCESSOR, purée asparagus tips. Melt the butter in a soup pot, add the leeks, and cook over moderate heat until softened, about 5 minutes. Add the asparagus tips, potatoes, stock, bay leaf, and bring to a boil. Reduce the heat to low and simmer until the potatoes are tender, about 15 minutes.

DISCARD BAY LEAF and, using an immersion blender, purée until smooth. You can also purée in batches using a traditional blender. Return to the pot and add milk, salt, and white pepper. Simmer for an additional 5 minutes. Taste again for seasoning. Ladle into soup bowls or serve cold and swirl in a spoonful of sour cream or yogurt.

Vichyssoise is traditionally a potato leek soup made with chicken stock, typically served cold. It is also a great base for the vegetables you have on hand to shine. I often have unused broccoli and asparagus in my refrigerator and always look to work them into my salvage dishes. What makes this version so flavorful is simmering the asparagus stems in the stock. If using broccoli, use the same technique and simmer the broccoli stems. The potatoes release starch into the soup, which lends a subtle thickening to the soup.

WILD MUSHROOM BISQUE

1 to 1½ pounds mushrooms, wiped clean with a towel, stems trimmed
1 shallot, minced
1 garlic clove, minced
3 sprigs thyme (leaves only)
2 tablespoons olive oil
Salt
2 tablespoons butter
1 leek, cleaned and cut into ½-inch slices (page 99)
1 onion, peeled and rough chopped
½ cup sherry
1 tablespoon porcini powder (optional)
2 quarts *Chicken Stock* (page 119)
1 cup milk
1 cup white mushrooms (about 4 ounces), sliced

PREHEAT OVEN TO 400°F.

COMBINE MUSHROOMS (except sliced mushrooms) with shallots, garlic, fresh thyme, oil, and 1 teaspoon of salt in a roasting pan. Mix well to coat the mushrooms and place in oven for 8 to 10 minutes until all vegetables are slightly brown.

IN A SOUP POT over medium heat, cook leeks and onions with 2 tablespoons of butter until soft (about 5 minutes). Add sherry and reduce until the alcohol has burned off, about 2 minutes.

ADD ROASTED MUSHROOMS (and the porcini powder) and vegetable stock and stir. Simmer for 40 minutes.

WHILE SOUP IS SIMMERING, cook the sliced mushrooms in a small amount of olive oil. Mushrooms should be slightly browned but not cooked for more than 2 to 3 minutes. Set aside.

PURÉE THE SOUP with immersion blender until smooth. Add milk and simmer for another 10 minutes. Taste for seasoning. Right before serving, stir in the sautéed mushrooms.

Mushrooms have a very short life in your refrigerator, so I like to roast them in garlic and thyme and then freeze them or make a rich aromatic pot of mushroom bisque. Bisque usually implies the use of cream but my version finishes with a small amount of milk. Use a combination of mushrooms or a single variety, depending on what you have on hand. I like to sauté a few sliced mushrooms and stir into the bisque right before serving.

Makes 2 quarts

VEGETARIAN FRENCH ONION SOUP

Another favorite at Epicure is my French onion soup. It is vegetarian, but is equally delicious with chicken or beef stock. I like combining red and white onions or mixing in shallots and leeks for variety. This recipe floats a smoky cheddar/Gruyère crostini on top of the soup but you can use any melting cheese and several-days old bread under the broiler.

Makes 2 quarts

2 tablespoons butter
1 tablespoon olive oil
2 white onions, peeled and sliced
1 red onion, peeled and sliced
1 shallot, peeled and sliced
2 teaspoons salt
4 sprigs of thyme
1 cup red wine
½ cup sherry
2 quarts *All-Natural Vegetable Stock* (page 117)
½ baguette, sliced (8 slices)
½ cup Gruyère, shredded
½ cup sharp cheddar, shredded
1 teaspoon smoked paprika
½ teaspoon dried thyme

PREHEAT OVEN TO 400°F.

IN A DUTCH OVEN, MELT BUTTER with olive oil over a medium heat. Place the onions, salt, and thyme in the pot and stir to coat the onions. Lower the heat, cover, and cook the onions slowly until deep golden in color, about 25 to 30 minutes. Stir frequently. If onions begin to brown or stick to the bottom, add ½ cup of vegetable stock.

WHEN ONIONS ARE CARAMELIZED AND THICK, add red wine and sherry and reduce liquid by half. Add vegetable stock and simmer for 20 minutes. Adjust seasoning to taste.

PLACE BAGUETTE SLICES on a baking sheet. Combine cheeses, paprika, and thyme. Sprinkle mixture generously on bread slices and bake for 3 to 4 minutes until melted and bubbling.

SPICY TOMATO GAZPACHO
with Lobster

My gazpacho is a bit chunky and has just the right amount of heat. I love shellfish with my gazpacho and you can substitute poached shrimp or cooked scallops for the lobster. Cold blender soups, like this one, use your best excess vegetables and fruit to their best advantage. Use any variety of tomato, onion, or pepper and adjust the spices to your taste.

Serves 4

- 2 lobster claws, steamed and taken out of the shell, sliced in half lengthwise (4 pieces)
- 1½ pounds tomatoes, seeded and rough chopped
- ¼ cup red onion, rough chopped
- ½ cucumber peeled, seeded and rough chopped
- ¼ cup red pepper, seeded and diced
- 1 garlic clove, minced
- 1 serrano chili, seeded and minced
- ½ lime, juiced
- 1 teaspoon Worcestershire sauce
- 1 teaspoon smoked paprika
- 1 teaspoon ground coriander
- ½ teaspoon salt
- ½ teaspoon black pepper
- 1 tablespoon olive oil
- 2 tablespoons fresh parsley, finely chopped

COMBINE ALL INGREDIENTS except parsley in a glass bowl, stir well. Measure 1 cup of the mixture and purée it in a food processor or blender and then return to the bowl. Taste for seasoning. Refrigerate until cold. Pour gazpacho into soup bowls, place a lobster claw piece in the middle, and garnish with chopped parsley.

Who doesn't love sandwiches? Sandwiches are attaining new status as the bread section of markets and bakeries expands. Sandwiches are also appearing on many upscale restaurant menus. My niece Casey, a recent Le Cordon Bleu grad is someone who knows a thing or two about sandwiches (www.anatomyofasandwich.com). She will tell you all one needs are a few ordinary ingredients to transform a piece of cooked fish or a leftover chicken breast into an extraordinary sandwich. Delicious bread, your favorite cheese, fresh herbs, pickled vegetables, bacon, crispy lettuce, paper-thin sliced onions, jalapeño peppers . . . most likely you won't have to look too far for these and other accompaniments to create a great tasting sandwich. In this chapter, I describe some of my favorite sandwiches, all utilizing one or more salvage ingredients from the kitchen. Fresh bread is always preferable, but when not available, toasting is fine.

CHAPTER 8: BETWEEN THE BREAD

Sandwichery at its Finest

TURKEY SLIDERS WITH
Broccoli Slaw

Turkey burgers have grown in popularity across the country but still seem to suffer from a common affliction no matter where you eat them: They Are Dry. Combining sautéed vegetables into your ground turkey or chicken will make your burgers tasty and moist. I always find a few salvage vegetables in the produce drawer and I experiment with whatever I have left in the jars on my refrigerator door (artichoke hearts, roasted peppers, etc.). The slaw is made from grating broccoli stems, carrots, and cabbage. Asparagus stems work as well. This is a great way to make use of stems on a vegetable whose tips or florets have been used for an earlier meal. You can use leftover coleslaw in place of the broccoli slaw.

Serves 3 (6 sliders)

BROCCOLI SLAW
4 broccoli stems, grated
1 carrot, grated
½ cup red or green cabbage, grated
¼ cup red onion, thinly sliced
3 tablespoons mayonnaise
1 lime, juiced and zested (about 2 tablespoons of juice and 1 teaspoon of zest)
1 teaspoon Dijon mustard
Salt and pepper

TOSS ALL THE SLAW INGREDIENTS in a medium-sized bowl until well combined. Refrigerate until ready to use.

ADD 1 TABLESPOON OF OIL in a pan over medium-high heat and add roasted pepper, artichoke hearts, olives, onions, garlic, and spice blend. Cook until soft, about 5 minutes. Stir frequently to avoid burning. Turn off heat and allow for the mixture to cool, about 10 minutes.

COMBINE GROUND TURKEY, cooked vegetables, ketchup, parsley, egg, Worcestershire sauce, mustard, dried oregano, and salt until evenly blended. Using wet hands, form 6 equal patties.

WIPE PAN USED FOR VEGETABLES with a sheet of paper towel and place over a medium-high heat. Add remaining 1 tablespoon of canola oil and when oil is hot and shimmering, place patties in the pan. Sear for

SLIDERS

2 tablespoons canola oil
1 roasted red pepper (from the jar)
3 artichoke hearts
2 tablespoons chopped olives
2 tablespoons red onion, chopped
1 garlic clove, minced
1 tablespoon *All-Purpose Love Rub* (page 29)
1 pound ground turkey
½ cup ketchup
½ cup parsley, finely chopped
1 egg
1 teaspoon Worcestershire sauce
1 teaspoon Dijon mustard
½ teaspoon dried oregano
1 tablespoon canola oil
1 to 2 tomatoes, thickly sliced (need 6 slices)
6 slider buns or hamburger rolls (lightly toasted)

3 minutes, careful not to burn. Turn down heat if browning too fast. Flip the burgers and cook second side for additional 3 minutes. Internal temperature should read 165°F.

PLACE A THICK TOMATO SLICE on each bun bottom to form a base for your slider. Top slider with a generous spoonful of slaw and follow with bun top to complete sandwich.

SUN-DRIED TOMATO AND PESTO GRILLED CHEESE
with Asiago

What's better than gooey cheese, tangy sun-dried tomatoes, and rich pesto on grilled bread? Asiago Pressato is a fresh cheese (not aged) that is one of the better melting cheeses. Mozzarella will work as well, and you can substitute fresh or roasted tomatoes for the sun-dried element. My bread of choice for this sandwich is ciabatta, a yeasty wheat bread that is airy on the inside and has a great exterior for toasting or grilling. Co-incidently, ciabatta was created about thirty years ago in Veneto, Italy, the same region that makes Asiago.

Serves 2

1 ciabatta loaf, sliced
  horizontally
¼ pound Asiago, sliced
½ cup sun-dried tomatoes
3 tablespoons pesto

SPREAD THE PESTO on both ciabatta halves. Layer Asiago on bottom half, followed by sun-dried tomatoes, and top with more Asiago. Complete the sandwich by placing the top half on the cheese layer.

ADD 2 TEASPOONS OF OLIVE OIL to a hot pan (cast-iron skillet or grill pan preferred) and place the sandwich carefully in the pan. Place either a heavy plate or pot on top of sandwich to create medium pressure. Cook for 2 minutes until golden brown. Pour another teaspoon of olive oil on top of the sandwich before flipping. Carefully flip the sandwich and cook another 2 minutes until second side is golden brown and cheese is oozing. Cut sandwich into 4-inch slices and serve immediately.

TURKEY BACON AND APPLE GRILLED CHEESE
with Cheddar and Gruyère

4 slices thick-cut egg bread (or other white or wheat bread cut into thick slices)
4 ounces sharp cheddar, sliced
4 ounces Gruyère, sliced
4 slices turkey bacon
1 tablespoon honey
¼ cup mustard (preferably whole grain mustard)
1 apple, cored, halved, and sliced into ¼-inch semi-circle slices
2 sprigs fresh thyme, leaves only
2 tablespoons olive oil

FOR SIMPLE GRILLED CHEESE: Use a favorite spread on your bread, then place slices of cheddar and Gruyère between the bread slices.

ADD 2 TEASPOONS OF OLIVE OIL to a hot pan (cast-iron skillet or grill pan preferred) and place the sandwich carefully in the pan. Place either a heavy plate or pot on top of sandwich to create medium pressure. Cook for 2 minutes until golden brown. Pour another teaspoon of olive oil on top of the sandwich before flipping. Carefully flip the sandwich and cook another 2 minutes until second side is golden brown and cheese is oozing. Cut sandwich in half and serve immediately.

FOR TURKEY BACON AND APPLE GRILLED CHEESE: Place 6 slices of turkey bacon on a baking sheet and place on the middle rack of a 400°F oven. Cook the bacon for 8 to 10 minutes or until crispy.

IN A SMALL BOWL mix honey and mustard together until well blended. Spread one side of each slice of bread with the mixture and arrange both cheeses on 2 of them, followed by the apple slices and cooked bacon. Place a few more slices of each cheese on top of the bacon, add a sprinkle of thyme, and close the sandwich with the other slice of bread. Grill as directed above.

These two sandwiches are inspired by my sister, Deb, who loves to have grilled cheese parties. Sometimes the best grilled cheese is simply a delicious combination of two cheeses: one mild melting cheese and the other, a sharp cheese with a slight salty bite. The pairing of Gruyère and cheddar is perfect. To take this grilled cheese to another level, add turkey bacon, a few slices of apple, a sprinkle of fresh thyme, and spread with chutney or homemade honey mustard.

Serves 2

SEARED AHI TUNA, AVOCADO,
Arugula with Mango Salsa

As a child, I grew up eating tuna salad made with lots of mayonnaise, chopped celery, and a squeeze of lemon. Now I prefer fresh tuna, quickly seared rare, chilled, and served with avocado and mango. Wasabi powder is a wonderful ingredient to have in your pantry. It gives your marinades and sauces a nice spicy kick, makes a tangy mayo that compliments fish or chicken, turns yogurt or sour cream into a flavorful condiment, and is a great addition to your homemade salad dressings in place of Dijon.

Makes 1 sandwich

2 tablespoons olive oil
5 ounces fresh tuna
Salt and black pepper
1 teaspoon wasabi powder
2 tablespoons mayonnaise
1 ciabatta roll (baguette or
  French bread)
½ lemon
½ cup arugula
¼ cup *Avocado, Cucumber,
  Tomato, and Mango Salsa*
  (page 113)
½ cup pickled vegetables

SPRINKLE TUNA ON BOTH SIDES with salt and pepper. Heat 2 tablespoons of olive oil in a non-stick pan until the oil begins to smoke.

SEAR THE TUNA over medium-high heat for 2 minutes. Carefully turn the fish and cook the second side for an additional 2 minutes. Remove the tuna from the pan and let cool on a plate for about 10 minutes. Place in the refrigerator for at least 1 hour before slicing.

BLEND MAYO AND WASABI POWDER in a small bowl with a small whisk or fork. When ready to serve, slice the tuna against the grain into ¼-inch slices. Squeeze lemon over the tuna slices and place on bottom half of baguette. Arrange arugula over the tuna and top with mango salsa. Smear wasabi mayo on other baguette half and place on top to complete the sandwich. Cut in half and serve with pickled vegetables.

POACHED CHICKEN BREAST
with Roasted Peppers, Basil, and Sun-dried Tomato Mayo

Poaching in white wine and herbs is healthier than cooking chicken in butter or oil. Poaching keeps the breasts moist and plump and you can use your favorite herbs to infuse the poaching liquid. You can poach the chicken ahead of time and keep in the freezer. I like dark bread for this sandwich, like a pumpernickel, olive bread, or raisin walnut (shown).

Makes 1 sandwich

3 sun-dried tomatoes, finely chopped
2 tablespoons mayonnaise
1 teaspoon olive oil
½ teaspoon *All-Purpose Love Rub* (page 29)
1 cup white wine
1 cup *Chicken Stock* (page 119), or water
1 boneless chicken breast (about 5 ounces)
½ onion, sliced
1 sprig rosemary
2 sage leaves
1 garlic clove, smashed
1 large roasted red pepper
5 basil leaves
2 slices raisin walnut bread (dark rye or pumpernickel)

BLEND SUN-DRIED TOMATOES, mayonnaise, olive oil, and spice blend with a small whisk or fork.

IN A MEDIUM-SIZED PAN, bring wine, chicken stock, onions, and herbs to a simmer. Sprinkle a generous amount of salt on both sides of chicken breast and place in the simmering liquid. Poach for 15 minutes until completely cooked through.

LIGHTLY TOAST the bread and smear the dressing on one side of both slices. Place the chicken cutlet on the toast and top with red pepper and basil leaves. Lay the other toast slice on top to complete the sandwich. Cut in half and serve.

OPEN-FACED CHICKEN SALAD
with Apples, Dried Cranberries, and Melted Brie

Leftover cooked chicken breast is typically dry and gets drier and less tasty as the days go on. This salvage sandwich transforms your leftover chicken, apples, celery, red onion, dried cranberries, and a wedge of brie into something memorable.

Makes 2 sandwiches

2 slices dark bread (wheat, pumpernickel, health bread, or brioche)
½ cup mayonnaise
½ lemon, juiced
2 teaspoons Dijon mustard
½ teaspoon dried thyme
12 ounces cooked chicken, rough chopped (see *Homemade Chicken Soup*—page 119)
2 celery stalks, diced
1 apple, cored and diced
2 tablespoons red onion, diced
¼ cup dried cranberries
2 teaspoon olive oil
Salt and black pepper
4 slices of brie

PREHEAT OVEN TO 400°F.

PLACE BREAD SLICES in the oven to slightly toast them (2 to 3 minutes).

COMBINE MAYONNAISE, LEMON JUICE, mustard, thyme, salt, and pepper. Mix well and then fold in chicken, celery, apples, red onion, and cranberries. Add olive oil and give another stir. Taste for seasoning.

PLACE HALF THE CHICKEN SALAD on each of the 2 slices of toast. Top each with brie slices and place in oven for 3 to 4 minutes to melt the cheese. Serve open-faced.

FISH SALAD SANDWICH
with Smoky Dill Dressing

Quite often I have a piece or two of leftover grilled or baked fish. Unfortunately, reheating fish tends to dry it out and microwaving robs it of any flavor or desirable texture. I like to make a fish salad (similar to a traditional tuna fish salad) out of my leftover fish by adding fresh herbs, vegetables on hand, and refrigerator-door ingredients.

Serves 2

10 ounces cooked fish
½ cup *Everything Sauce* (page 49), plus 2 tablespoons for spreading on toast
¼ cup cornichons (or other pickles on hand), finely chopped
1 handful (about 1/3 cup) fresh dill, finely chopped
½ red onion, sliced
4 slices wheat bread (or dark, rye, pumpernickel, white)

PREHEAT OVEN TO 400°F.

COMBINE SAUCE, PICKLES, AND DILL in a bowl until blended. Break apart fish into small pieces and fold into dressing.

LIGHTLY TOAST BREAD SLICES (about 2 minutes) and then spread sauce on one side of all slices. Place a scoop (about 6 to 7 ounces) of fish salad on 2 toast slices and arrange a layer of red onion slices. Top with remaining toast slices to complete sandwich. Cut in half and serve.

TALEGGIO-STUFFED BRISKET BURGER
with Caramelized Onions

1½ pounds ground brisket, formed into 8 patties (about 3 ounces each)
6 ounces Taleggio cheese, cut into 2 by 2-inch squares
Salt and pepper
1 red onion sliced
1 tablespoon butter
1 tablespoon olive oil
1 teaspoon anchovy paste
1 tablespoon canola oil
2 tablespoons mayonnaise
2 teaspoons *Savory Spice Blend* (page 32)
1 teaspoon white horseradish
4 hamburger buns

PLACE A SLICE OF CHEESE on top of 4 of the patties and top each of them with another patty, forming a "patty sandwich." Gently press the patties together (to about 1½ inches thick) and pinch the edges to seal the patty. No cheese should be showing. Sprinkle both sides of each patty with salt and black pepper.

HEAT BUTTER AND OIL in a heavy-bottomed pan over medium heat until butter is bubbly but not brown. Add onions and anchovy paste and cook for 10 minutes until light brown and caramelized. Remove onions to a bowl and cover to keep warm.

WIPE OUT THE PAN with a sheet of paper towel and place over a medium-high heat. Add 1 tablespoon of canola oil and when oil is hot and shimmering, place burgers in the pan. Sear for 2 minutes and flip the burgers. Cook second side for additional 2 minutes.

COMBINE MAYONNAISE, spice blend, and horseradish until blended.

LIGHTLY TOAST BUNS and spread with mayonnaise mixture. Arrange a thin layer of lettuce on the bottoms of hamburger buns and place burgers on lettuce, followed by caramelized onions. Place tops on the onions to complete the sandwich.

Everyone has an opinion on what cut of meat makes the best burger. Brisket meat is my favorite because it has the right fat content (about 15 to 20 percent) and will give your burger flavor and juiciness. This burger is stuffed with Taleggio, a strong and flavorful soft-rind cheese, and topped with sweet caramelized onions. You can use any cheese you have on hand to stuff your burger.

Serves 4

CHAPTER 9: VERSATILE AND VEGETARIAN

Entrées for the Veggie Crowd

An increasing number of Americans now categorize themselves as Occasional Vegetarians, joining the growing number of vegetarians and vegans in the country. I suspect one of the reasons my Epicure with Love soups at Epicure are so popular is because they are made with vegetable stock.

One of the most common items in our refrigerators is leftover cooked vegetables. Often they can be revived simply with a fresh sprig of thyme or a scoop of plain yogurt. I also like to combine fresh vegetables with canned or jar vegetables from the pantry.

VEGETARIAN MEDITERRANEAN FRITTATA

This frittata is packed with flavors from the Mediterranean. Go easy on the salt as the capers and olives have a good amount of saltiness. The cucumber sour cream is a great dip for fresh veggies as well as a fine accompaniment to fish.

Serves 4 to 6

**CUCUMBER
SOUR CREAM**
½ cup sour cream
½ cucumber, peeled,
    seeded, and rough
    chopped
1 teaspoon lemon juice
1 teaspoon olive oil

FRITTATA
8 eggs
½ cup milk
2 tablespoons heavy cream
½ teaspoon red chili flakes
1 garlic clove, peeled and
    minced
1 tablespoon capers, drained
1 tablespoon olives, pitted
    and sliced
¼ cup artichoke hearts
¼ cup sun-dried tomatoes,
    drained and chopped
4 ounces feta cheese,
    crumbled
Salt and pepper, to taste

PREHEAT OVEN TO 400°F.

CUCUMBER SOUR CREAM

PLACE CUCUMBER CHUNKS in a mini food processor with lemon juice and 2 teaspoons of olive oil, then pulse until puréed but still slightly chunky. Pour into a small bowl, add sour cream, and stir. Season with salt and pepper.

FRITTATA

WHISK TOGETHER EGGS, milk, cream, feta, and season with a pinch of salt. Add ¼ teaspoon of black pepper if you like. There is plenty of salt from the capers and olives, so you don't want to overdo it.

PLACE A 10-INCH NON-STICK SKILLET over a medium heat and add 2 tablespoons of olive oil. Add chili flakes to hot oil and then after 20 seconds add sun-dried tomatoes, artichoke hearts, capers, and olives. Stir frequently for 2 minutes to soften the vegetables without browning them. Add garlic and stir for another 20 seconds.

POUR EGG MIXTURE INTO PAN and stir well. Using a spatula, pull the egg mixture from the edges of the pan and from the bottom. When egg mixture is partially "set," place in the oven for 10 minutes until frittata puffs up and the top is lightly browned. Slide a knife around the edge of the pan to loosen the frittata. Slide frittata onto a cutting board and cut into 6 or 8 wedges. Serve with cucumber sour cream.

Creative uses . . .

- *Cooked vegetables and meat or chicken from last night's dinner make an excellent frittata filling. Start with a sautéed shallot or small onion, add cooked vegetables and meat or chicken for 2 to 3 minutes to warm through. Pour in egg mixture and continue with recipe. Add some fresh herbs and crumble your favorite cheese on the frittata when it comes out of the oven.*
- *Add canned beans or peas with some fresh herbs to sautéed spinach or mushrooms. Spoonfuls of goat cheese or ricotta go well with these combinations.*
- *If you have leftover cooked ground meat (beef, chicken, or turkey), add to a hot pan to warm through, sprinkle with your favorite dried herbs or spice blend, and add eggs.*
- *Cooked potatoes are delicious with sautéed onions and fresh thyme or rosemary.*

VEGETARIAN CHILI

When I launched the Epicure with Love line of soups at the Epicure Gourmet Markets in November 2011, the Big Bold Chili with Prime Beef and Italian Sausage was an instant hit. Soon after, customers asked for a vegetarian version. This vegetarian chili uses roasted mushrooms to mimic the texture of ground beef and the roasted vegetables give great depth of flavor. Don't worry if you don't have all the vegetables listed. As always, use what you have on hand.

Makes 2 quarts

- 4 ounces mushrooms, finely chopped
- 2 tablespoon olive oil
- Salt and pepper
- 2 carrots, diced
- 3 zucchini, peeled, seeded and diced
- 3 yellow squash, seeded and diced
- 2 onion, diced
- 2 garlic cloves, minced
- 1 red pepper, seeded and diced
- ½ poblano pepper or jalapeño, seeded and minced (optional)
- 4 tablespoons *Chili Spice Blend* (page 31)
- 1 can of beer (12-ounce)
- 12 ounces *Vegetable Stock* (page 117)
- 1 (14-ounce) can whole tomatoes
- 2 tablespoons tomato paste
- 1 (14-ounce) can pinto beans, drained and rinsed

PREHEAT OVEN TO 400°F.

SCATTER FINELY CHOPPED MUSHROOMS on a baking sheet and drizzle with 1 tablespoon of olive oil. Season with salt and pepper. Place in oven and roast for 5 minutes or until mushrooms begin to brown. Be careful not to let mushrooms burn. Remove from pan and set aside.

PLACE CARROTS, ZUCCHINI, AND SQUASH in same roasting pan and drizzle with 1 tablespoon of oil. Season with salt and pepper. Place in oven and roast for 15 minutes or until vegetables are slightly browned on the edges.

HEAT 1 TABLESPOON OF OLIVE OIL in a 4-quart heavy bottomed pot over medium-high heat. Add onions and cook to soften without browning, about 5 minutes. Add garlic, stir, and cook for an additional 2 minutes.

ADD PEPPERS, ROASTED VEGETABLES, roasted mushrooms, and spice blend. Cook for 5 to 8 minutes to soften the peppers and toast the spices. Pour in beer to deglaze. When alcohol has burned off (2 minutes), add the stock, tomatoes, tomato paste, and beans.

CONTINUE TO STIR and bring the chili to a simmer. Simmer for 45 minutes, stirring frequently. Taste for seasoning.

RED QUINOA WITH AVOCADO, CHICKPEAS,
and Dried Apricots

Known to the Incas as the "mother of all grains," quinoa (pronounced keen-wah) has twice the protein of rice and combines well with so many different ingredients due to its neutral flavor. Quinoa comes in many different types and colors. At Epicure, we use a lot of red quinoa because of its beautiful rich color. This delicious recipe uses a tri-color grain, is low in fat, and has a healthy combination of protein and carbs. Use raisins, cranberries, or any dried fruit in place of apricots as well as whatever variety of cooked beans you have in your pantry.

Serves 4

1 cup quinoa
1 lemon, juiced and zested (about 2 tablespoons of juice and 1 teaspoon of zest)
1 lime, juiced and zested (about 2 tablespoons of juice and 1 teaspoon of zest)
½ teaspoon red chili flake
2 teaspoons *Savory Spice Blend* (page 32)
Salt and pepper
1 (14-ounce) can chickpeas, drained and rinsed
1 avocado, diced
½ cup dried apricots, halved
¼ cup fresh cilantro, finely chopped (or parsley)

BRING 2 CUPS OF WATER to a boil, add 1 tablespoon of salt, and cook quinoa according to the package. When water is fully absorbed, use a fork and fluff the quinoa. Let cool.

IN A SMALL BOWL, blend juice and zest from lemon and lime, red chili flake, spice blend, ½ teaspoon of salt, and ¼ teaspoon of black pepper. In a large salad bowl, combine the chickpeas, avocado, and apricots. Add the cooled quinoa, dressing, and chopped cilantro. Gently stir all ingredients together. Taste and adjust seasoning with spice blend.

GRILLED TOFU STEAK
with Thyme Honey Mustard

I have to say that I have not been a fan of tofu but it was recently my good fortune to try a seared tofu "steak" that my photographer, Lynn, marinated overnight in honey mustard. I discovered the secret to preparing a delicious tofu "steak" is to create a dry texture on the inside and a crispy sear on the outside. This pan-roasted recipe is absolutely fantastic with the addition of fresh thyme and works with a variety of dressings and marinades (see Marinades—page 37).

Serves 4

1 block of firm tofu (1 pound)
¼ cup Dijon mustard
¼ cup honey
5 to 6 sprigs fresh thyme
1 tablespoon olive oil
1 tablespoon salt
1 tablespoon canola oil

MAKE THE MARINADE by blending mustard, honey, fresh thyme, and olive oil.

DRAIN THE WATER out of the tofu package and gently press between sheets of paper towel. Slice in half horizontally and then carefully slice in half again, forming 4½-inch "steaks." Sprinkle with salt, cover with dry paper towel, and refrigerate for an hour. Remove the paper towel and place in a shallow dish and cover with half the marinade. Turn several times to coat all sides. Cover with plastic wrap and refrigerate for several hours, if possible.

HEAT A NON-STICK PAN OR GRIDDLE over medium heat and add 1 tablespoon of oil. When oil is hot and shimmering, gently place tofu slices in the pan. Sear for 2 minutes and flip. Sear for additional 2 minutes and then lower the heat for 15 minutes. Brush on additional marinade several times throughout cooking and flip steaks periodically to cook out the internal moisture.

REMOVE FROM PAN, BRUSH ON MARINADE one last time and serve immediately.

Creative uses . . .

- *By combining tofu with rice, quinoa, or whole grain couscous, you have a complete protein and a delicious and nutritious meal. Make some extra marinade and pour it over the rice and sprinkle with chopped parsley.*
- *You can also make a tofu steak sandwich in a pita with fresh chopped tomatoes and* Everything Sauce *(page 49).*
- *Serve with a vegetable or salad. You can slice the cooked tofu into 1-inch cubes and then toss into roasted or sautéed vegetables. I enjoy them in a salad, using the honey mustard as a salad dressing. Simply blend in a tablespoon of cider vinegar to the honey mustard mixture.*
- *Soy sauce pairs well with tofu. Be careful not to over-salt the tofu when using soy sauce. Add a tablespoon of brown sugar and a drizzle of oyster sauce (optional) to the soy sauce. This makes a nice sticky glaze that is both salty and sweet and goes wonderfully with roasted sweet potatoes or chopped scallions. Other additions to your soy-glazed tofu can include a handful of bean sprouts or a spoonful of crushed nuts.*
- *If you have a panini press, you can cut the cooking time in half. Make sure you spray both sides of the press with cooking spray so the tofu doesn't stick, and keep the temperature at medium throughout.*

POLENTA WITH ROASTED TOMATOES
and Wild Mushroom Ragu

¾ cup polenta (not instant)
1½ cup *Vegetable Stock* (page 117)
Salt
1 cup *Roasted Tomatoes* (page 54)
1 tablespoon butter
2 tablespoon olive oil
½ pound mushrooms (wild, if available)
1 shallot, minced
2 sprigs fresh thyme
Salt and pepper
1 tablespoon parsley, finely chopped

BRING VEGETABLE STOCK TO A BOIL and add a generous amount of salt (about 1 tablespoon). Whisk in the polenta until no lumps appear and then lower the heat to a low simmer. Stir frequently with a wooden spoon and cook for 15 to 20 minutes. If polenta gets too thick, add a little more stock.

TO PREPARE MUSHROOMS, place a large pan on medium-high heat and add a tablespoon each of butter and olive oil. Once the butter is bubbly but not brown, add mushrooms to the pan and spread out in one layer. Drizzle another tablespoon of olive oil over them and do not stir or shake the pan. After 2 minutes, move the mushrooms around with a wooden spoon and add the shallots, thyme, salt, and pepper. Cook for 1 minute longer, stirring constantly.

TO ASSEMBLE THE DISH, fold the warm mushrooms into the polenta and place a large spoonful in a ramekin or bowl. Top with warm roasted tomatoes and chopped parsley.

Creative uses . . .

- *For a non-vegan version, stir in ¼ cup of mascarpone cheese and ¼ cup of grated Pecorino Romano into the polenta when it is finished cooking.*
- *Use fresh herbs like chervil, basil, sage, and rosemary. Finely chop the herbs and fold into the polenta just before serving.*
- *For a firm polenta dish, spray a sheet of plastic wrap with cooking spray and pour cooled polenta in the middle. Form an 8-inch log and roll the polenta in the plastic wrap. Twist at both ends and refrigerate for at least 2 hours. Remove from refrigerator, unwrap and slice into 1-inch wheels. You can sear the plain polenta wheels in a hot pan or bread them first with panko.*

Many diners have enjoyed eating polenta at a restaurant but haven't tried to make it at home. You may be familiar with the type of firm polenta that is cooked and chilled, then sliced and seared. You may also have tasted its creamier cousin, which has a texture closer to a purée. This recipe offers a soft and creamy cornmeal side dish complemented with tangy tomatoes that contrast well with the natural sweetness of the corn. The wild mushrooms lend an earthy flavor and texture. Slow-cooking polenta is preferred but you can use instant polenta as long as you continue to add liquid for the right consistency.

Serves 4

ROASTED ROOT VEGETABLES
with Brown Rice

My mother and my sister have a favorite vegetable dish that has also become a favorite of mine. Slow roasting in a little bit of olive oil, salt, and fresh herbs produces the most flavorful vegetables. I roast broccoli this way almost every night for Michele and the kids and we frequently add green beans, Brussels sprouts, cauliflower, sweet potatoes, and whatever else that is hiding in the produce drawer. This recipe uses leftover brown rice and a spoonful of yogurt.

Serves 4

1 pound sweet potatoes and/or butternut squash

3 parsnips, peeled and cut into ½-inch pieces

½ pound baby carrots, stem left on

½ pound Brussels sprouts, trimmed and cut in half

3 medium-sized beets, peeled and quartered (about ¾ pound)

½ red onion, skin on and quartered

6 garlic cloves, skin on and smashed

5 to 6 thyme sprigs

¼ cup olive oil

Salt

2 cups leftover rice

¼ cup plain yogurt

PREHEAT OVEN TO 400°F.
Place all vegetables and thyme in a large roasting pan. Sprinkle generously with salt and pour olive oil over the vegetables. Toss to coat all the vegetables, place in the oven, and roast for 45 minutes, occasionally turning and moving them around. (If you don't want your vegetables to turn light purple from the beets, roast the beets separately.)

REHEAT LEFTOVER RICE IN A STEAMER or place rice in a baking pan with a few tablespoons of water, cover tightly with foil, and bake in the oven for 10 minutes until warmed through and fluffy. Serve vegetables over the rice and add a dollop of yogurt on top.

VEGETABLE COCONUT CURRY

1 onion, sliced
2 garlic cloves, minced
1 teaspoon ginger, minced
1 tablespoon red curry paste
12 ounces coconut milk
8 ounces *Vegetable Stock* (page 117)
½ red pepper, seeded and cut into strips
½ green pepper, seeded and cut into strips
½ orange pepper, seeded and cut into strips
2 tablespoons brown sugar
1 tablespoon soy sauce
½ lime, juiced
6 basil leaves, chopped (plus 2 or 3 leaves for garnish)
2 cups leftover rice

IN A LARGE PAN, heat oil over a medium-high heat until shimmering. Add onions and cook for 2 minutes. Add curry paste, garlic, and ginger and continue cooking for another 2 minutes, stirring frequently. Do not burn the garlic.

ADD COCONUT MILK and stock and simmer for 2 minutes. Add peppers and continue simmering for 3 to 4 more minutes to soften the peppers. Add brown sugar, soy sauce, lime juice, and chopped basil. Stir until brown sugar is dissolved and remove from heat.

REHEAT LEFTOVER RICE IN A STEAMER or place rice in a baking pan with a few tablespoons of water, cover tightly with foil, and bake in the oven for 10 minutes until warmed through and fluffy.

Serve curry vegetables over the rice and garnish with basil leaves.

Creative uses . . .

- *For the non-vegetarians, add cooked chicken, pork, duck, turkey, beef, or fish during the last 3 to 4 minutes of cooking to warm through.*
- *Raw shrimp or scallops can be added during the last 2 minutes.*
- *Use broccoli, cauliflower, carrots, potatoes, string beans, sprouts, and any other vegetables you have on hand.*
- *Noodles are a nice variation. If you don't have rice noodles, use spaghetti or angel hair pasta. This is a great addition if you have leftover pasta.*

One of the most popular cuisines in Miami is Thai food. Whenever I go to a Thai restaurant or order in, my usual dish is a curry. This vegetarian curry dish is a simple curry with coconut milk and a touch of soy sauce and makes great use of onions, peppers, and your excess vegetables. Always start out with less curry paste as different brands have different levels of heat. You can always add more if you want it hotter.

Serves 4

VEGETARIAN CHOPPED "NOT" LIVER

I grew up eating chopped liver almost every Sunday at my grandmother's apartment and on all Jewish holidays. This was her version of hors d'oeuvres, along with pickled herring and gefilte fish served with red horseradish. I loved it all. At Epicure, chopped liver is a tradition and a deli case staple. I decided to try a vegetarian version and my mother shared a recipe that uses walnuts and peas. My version uses toasted pine nuts and I've added chickpeas to the green peas for a little firmer texture. The addition of honey is for Epicure fans, since the original Epicure chopped liver recipe uses honey for a touch of sweetness. Use pinto beans, navy beans, or any white beans in place of the chickpeas. This dish tastes better on the second day.

Makes 3 pounds

2 (12-ounce) cans green peas, drained and rinsed
1 (12-ounce) can chickpeas, drained and rinsed
5 eggs, hard boiled and peeled
2 onions, chopped
1 tablespoon olive oil
2 tablespoons honey
1/3 cup pine nuts, toasted

HEAT OIL IN A LARGE PAN over medium-high heat. When oil is shimmering, add onions. Turn down the heat to medium and cook onions until light brown and cara-melized, about 15 minutes. Take off the heat and allow to cool.

IN A FOOD PROCESSOR, COMBINE ALL INGREDI-ENTS. You will need to scrape down the sides several times. Continue to pulse until consistency reaches that of a purée.

Serve with crackers, celery or carrot sticks, endive, or hard boiled eggs.

CHAPTER 10: FROM SEA TO SHINING SEA

Fish and Seafood Entrées

ASIAN GINGER SALMON

Salmon is an extremely versatile fish and can be prepared many ways. You can grill it, roast it, bake it, poach it, or cook it on a stove top. My good friend Rudi (Epicure's meat manager) asked me to make an Asian marinade similar to a commercial product he was using on salmon for several customers. After some experimentation, we bottled my version for Epicure and now use it to prepare sides of salmon for customers who are looking for a sweet and spicy tanginess. Rudi added the sesame seeds, which produced a nutty flavor and texture that was absolutely perfect for the dish. Marinade can be made ahead of time.

Serves 4

4 salmon filets (skin off, 5 to 6 ounces each)
2 teaspoons salt
3 tablespoons of sesame seeds (white or black or both)
¼ cup *Asian Ginger Marinade* (page 43)

PREHEAT OVEN TO 375°F.

SPRINKLE BOTH SIDES OF FILETS generously with salt. Place filets in a baking dish and pour marinade over them. Cover with plastic wrap and refrigerate for an hour. Remove from refrigerator and sprinkle sesame seeds over the filets.

GENTLY PRESS SEEDS INTO THE FISH. Place in the oven and bake for 10 to 14 minutes (10 minutes for 1-inch filets, and 12 to 14 minutes for 1½ to 2-inch filets). Fish will be cooked to about medium and the top of the fish will be bubbly but not brown. For well-done fish, bake for an additional 2 to 3 minutes.

Fish, like all proteins, are best when fresh. While two to three-day-old fish isn't always considered fresh, it is still edible and delicious in most cases. I have divided this chapter into two categories: the first is fresh fish recipes that use salvage ingredients to complete the dish, and the second is salvaging leftover fish using fresh and salvage ingredients.

STEAMED LITTLENECK CLAMS
with Bok Choy in Chorizo Ginger Broth

One of the best dinners I ever cooked was a spur of the moment bowl of steamed clams for Michele and me. I bought fresh seafood to make seafood paella and as I was getting ready to prepare the dish, I realized I didn't have enough time. Taking inspiration from a number of ingredients I had on hand—chorizo in the freezer, a nub of ginger, garlic and onions, a few stalks of celery, and leftover bok choy—I decided to make a flavorful broth. Adding the fresh clams, shrimp, scallops, and a couple of small lobster tails I had bought for the paella, this dish came together in literally 15 minutes. The chorizo and spice blend are reminiscent of Spanish cooking and I think it's perfect for an appetizer or entrée. Michele absolutely loves it as a meal, served with crusty bread and a bottle of full-bodied red wine.

Serves 2

1 tablespoon olive oil
½ teaspoon red chili flake
½ cup chorizo, sliced
2 garlic cloves
1 small onion, diced
2 celery stalks, sliced
1 nub of ginger root, (about 1 inch) peeled and sliced
1 tablespoon *Spanish Spice Blend* (page 35), plus one teaspoon for finishing the dish
1 cup white wine
1 dozen littleneck clams
6 scallops
6 jumbo shrimp, peeled and deveined
3 small lobster tails, split down the middle of the underside of the tail
6 leaves bok choy, white and green parts, rough chopped
¼ cup parsley, chopped

IN A LARGE PAN, heat oil over a medium-high heat. Add chili flake and chorizo and cook for 2 minutes as the fat begins to render from the chorizo. Add garlic, onions, celery, ginger, and 2 teaspoons of spice blend. Cook for another 3 minutes to soften the vegetables.

ADD WINE, CLAMS, AND SCALLOPS. Sprinkle with another teaspoon of spice blend, give the pan a gentle shake, cover, and simmer until clams open (about 8 minutes). Add shrimp, lobster tails split side down, bok choy, and sprinkle with another teaspoon of spice blend. Cover and take off heat for 5 to 7 minutes to steam the lobster and bok choy.

DISCARD ANY UNOPENED CLAMS and, using a slotted spoon, scoop out the opened clams, scallops, shrimp, lobster tails, bok choy, and chorizo and arrange in serving bowls. Carefully pour broth over the seafood and sprinkle with fresh chopped parsley and one final dusting of spice blend.

HAWAIIAN SWORDFISH KEBOBS
with Pineapple

Kebobs are a great way to prepare fish such as swordfish, salmon, and halibut. A grilled fish kebob also sears more quickly on the grill than a single thick-cut fish filet. I like to skewer fruit with firm fish, and pineapple goes perfectly with swordfish, especially with a sweet and salty marinade. Add peppers, zucchini, or any other firm vegetable that not only adds color and flavor but will help keep the fish from sliding off the skewer.

Serves 4 (2 skewers per person)

1½ pounds swordfish, cut into 2-inch chunks (or other firm fish)

3 cups (2-inch) pineapple chunks

1 cup *Hawaiian Fish Marinade* (page 47)

1 green zucchini, cut into 2-inch chunks

1 yellow squash, cut into 2-inch chunks

2 red bell peppers, deseeded and sliced into 2-inch by 2-inch pieces

8 (8-inch) skewers (wooden or metal)

PLACE SWORDFISH CHUNKS IN MARINADE for 30 minutes.

TO PREPARE SKEWERS, start with yellow squash and slide until 1 inch from flat end of skewer. Follow with zucchini, then red pepper, swordfish, and pineapple. Continue alternating red pepper, swordfish, and pineapple and finish with a chunk of yellow squash.

AFTER LIGHTLY GREASING THE GRILL GRATES, grill skewers for 6 to 8 minutes over a medium-high heat, rotating frequently. Brush with marinade while grilling.

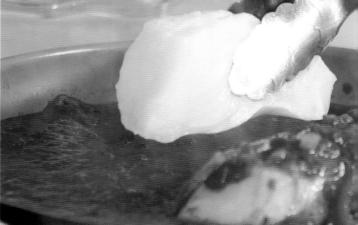

POACHED MARINATED SEA BASS ARRABIATA

Serves 2

2 (6-ounce) sea bass filets
2 tablespoon salt
2 lime, juiced
2 tablespoons olive oil
1 teaspoon red chili flake
2 garlic cloves, peeled and
    sliced thin
1 tablespoon capers, drained
    and rinsed
½ red onion, peeled and
    sliced
1 red bell pepper, deseeded
    and cut into strips
½ cup white wine
2 tablespoon salsa (choose
    based on your desired
    level of heat)
1 (14-ounce) can whole
    tomatoes
Salt and black pepper

PREPARE THE FISH by placing fish filets in a bowl and sprinkling salt on all sides. Squeeze lime juice over fish, cover bowl with plastic wrap, and refrigerate for 30 minutes.

IN A DEEP SKILLET, heat olive oil over medium-high heat. Add chili flake and garlic, and cook for 1 minute, stirring constantly to prevent garlic from burning. Add capers, onions, and peppers and toss to coat thoroughly. Cook for 5 minutes, careful not to brown the vegetables.

ADD WINE and stir up any brown bits on the bottom of skillet. Add salsa and stir. Lastly, add tomatoes by carefully squeezing each tomato in your hand as you toss them in the pan and pour in the remaining juice from can. Bring mixture to a simmer and add both fish filets. Cover and poach the fish for 8 to 10 minutes. Fish is done when a fork passes all the way through the filet with little resistance.

PLACE FISH ON A PLATTER and spoon the tomato mixture on top. Garnish with cilantro (or parsley) if serving it by itself. If serving with rice, parsley is the better option.

This is one of my favorite ways to enjoy sea bass, although you can use halibut, grouper, or monkfish as well. The sauce has a spicy kick, great depth of flavor, and uses up the last bit of onions, peppers, and garlic. Capers, salsa, and canned tomatoes are also incorporated, making it a perfect poaching liquid for cooking fish.

MIXED FISH CROQUETTES
with Roasted Red Pepper Mayo

This recipe came about at Epicure one day when Rudi received a duplicate fish order, resulting in an excess of fresh fish for the retail seafood case. We took a total of 30 pounds of salmon, mahi, grouper, and tilapia and cooked them in the steamer while we roasted a mixture of red onions, red and yellow bell peppers, and garlic. The cooked fish and vegetables were combined with spices, fresh herbs, and other accompaniments that transformed 30 pounds of excess fish into 45 pounds of delicious fish croquettes, which are now a weekly staple in the cooked foods section of the Epicure markets. This recipe is my favorite version of fish croquettes and you can use any fresh or cooked fish.

Serves 4

1 bell pepper (red, yellow or orange), diced
½ red onion, diced
2 garlic cloves, minced
2 tablespoons olive oil
2 teaspoons salt
1½ pounds cooked fish (or fresh fish, see page 179), broken into small pieces
1½ cup plain breadcrumbs (or panko)
½ cup ketchup
½ cup mayonnaise
1 egg
1 teaspoon dried basil
1 teaspoon dried oregano
½ teaspoon hot sauce (optional)
1 tablespoon Worcestershire sauce
1 teaspoon Dijon mustard
3 tablespoons *All-Purpose Love Rub* (page 29)
2 tablespoons canola oil
2 tablespoons roasted red pepper, finely chopped

PREHEAT OVEN TO 375°F.

PLACE DICED VEGETABLES IN A BAKING PAN, drizzle with olive oil, sprinkle with salt, toss to combine, and roast for 15 minutes until slightly brown. Remove from oven and allow vegetables to cool, about 10 minutes.

PLACE FISH IN A MEDIUM-SIZED BOWL and add vegetables, ½ cup of the breadcrumbs, ketchup, ¼ cup of the mayonnaise, egg, basil, oregano, hot sauce,

Worcestershire sauce, mustard, and 1 tablespoon of spice blend. Using your hands, mix thoroughly. Cover tightly with plastic wrap and refrigerate for 2 hours.

BLEND REMAINING 1 CUP OF BREADCRUMBS with 1 tablespoon of spice blend. Form 4 (6-ounce) "patties" out of the fish mixture and press each side gently into the seasoned breadcrumbs.

HEAT OIL IN A NON-STICK PAN over a medium-high heat. Brown the patties on both sides (about 2 minutes per side) and place on a baking sheet. Finish by baking patties in the oven for 6 to 8 minutes.

COMBINE REMAINING ¼ CUP MAYONNAISE with chopped pepper and remaining 1 tablespoon of spice blend. Serve with fish cakes.

IF USING FRESH FISH, sprinkle fish with salt and spice rub or Old Bay seasoning (about 1 teaspoon of each), and steam for 10 minutes until cooked through. If using an oven, place in a baking dish with ½ cup water and cover tightly with foil. Bake for 10 minutes. Allow fish to cool (about 15 minutes) before handling.

COD AND SCALLOP FRITTERS

1 bell pepper (red, yellow, or orange), diced
1 zucchini, diced
1 yellow squash, diced
½ red onion, diced
2 garlic cloves, minced
2 tablespoons olive oil
2 teaspoons salt
1 cup flour
1 teaspoon baking powder
1 tablespoon *Southern Spice Blend* (page 33)
2 eggs
½ cup cold water
1 pound cooked cod or any white flakey fish (if using fresh fish, page 179)
½ pound fresh scallops (or shrimp), cut into ½-inch pieces

PREHEAT OVEN TO 375°F.

PLACE DICED VEGETABLES in a roasting pan, drizzle with oil, sprinkle with salt, toss to combine, and roast until slightly brown, about 14 minutes. Remove from oven and allow vegetables to cool, about 10 minutes.

WHISK FLOUR, BAKING POWDER, AND SPICE BLEND in a large bowl. Add eggs and cold water and switching to a wooden spoon, blend the ingredients until you have a thick batter. Fold in cooked vegetables, fish, and scallops. Stir to combine.

HEAT VEGETABLE OIL in a medium-sized pot (about 3 to 4 inches) to 350°F. Carefully drop heaping tablespoons of batter into the oil, but don't crowd the pot (about 6 to 8 fritters at a time). Fry for 4 to 5 minutes until golden brown and crispy. Using a slotted spoon, remove the fritters to a paper towel-lined plate. Sprinkle with extra spice blend. Continue cooking the rest of the batter in batches. Serve warm with tartar sauce, *Everything Sauce* (page 49), or *Chili Mayo* (page 104).

Creative uses . . .

- *Replace cod and scallops with any cooked leftover fish or seafood and some fresh chopped herbs.*
- *The batter is quite versatile and can be used on a griddle for a pancake. Try a "fish griddle cake" by pouring batter on a hot, lightly greased griddle or non-stick pan. Cook similar to a pancake, flipping them once bubbles come to the surface.*
- *For a delicious side dish, add cooked leftover vegetables to this batter (no fish) and pour into greased ramekins or muffin tins. Cook for 12 minutes at 350°F until puffed and golden brown.*

This delicious fritter has a light texture from the flaked fish and a sweet roasted flavor from the vegetables. The scallops (which can be substituted with shrimp, conch, or lobster) give a contrasting firm texture in the fritter that lends balance and flavor.

Serves 4

SAN FRANCISCO FISH STEW

Sometimes referred to as Cioppino, this soup came from local fishermen's daily catch, which they "chopped" into the soup. You can add chunks of cooked fish in the last 5 minutes of the cooking process or sear fresh fish filets and add them when plating. This recipe really brings out the natural fish flavors, especially when you make your own stock.

Serves 4

SEAFOOD STOCK
2 tablespoons olive oil
1 onion, peeled and rough chopped
2 garlic cloves, chopped
1 carrot, peeled and rough chopped
2 celery stalks, rough chopped
3 sprigs of thyme
1 bay leaf
½ teaspoon red chili flake
6 cups water
Shrimp shells and tails (see Fish Stew)

IN A STOCKPOT, heat olive oil over a medium heat and add onion. Slowly cook to soften without browning, about 5 minutes. Stir in garlic for 1 minute. Add carrot, celery, thyme, bay leaf, and chili flake and continue cooking an additional 5 minutes. Stir frequently and turn down heat if necessary so vegetables don't brown. Add water and shrimp shells and tails and bring to boil. Skim the surface and lower the heat. Simmer for 20 minutes. Strain and keep stock warm.

FISH STEW

2 tablespoons olive oil
1 teaspoon red chili flake
2 sprigs fresh thyme
1 onion, peeled and rough chopped
1 shallot, peeled and sliced
2 garlic cloves, peeled and smashed
1 tablespoon flour
1 to 2 cups wine (red if using tomatoes, white if not)
4 cups seafood stock (or store bought seafood or chicken stock)
1 (14-ounce) can whole tomatoes (optional)
2 bay leaves
1 dozen littleneck clams
1 dozen mussels
4 sea scallops, cut in half

8 shrimp, peeled and deveined (save shrimp
shells and tails for stock)
4 cooked fish filets, about 1½ pounds
(if using fresh fish filets, see page 184)
Salt and black pepper

IN A STOCKPOT, heat olive oil, chili flake, and thyme over a medium heat for about
1 minute to infuse oil with flavors. Add onion, shallot, and garlic into the pot and
cook slowly to soften without browning, about 5 minutes. Stir in flour for 1 minute to
cook out the flour taste then add wine, stock, tomatoes, and bay leaf. Simmer for 30
minutes.

WITH 5 MINUTES REMAINING, add the clams, mussels, and scallops. When the
shellfish have opened, add the shrimp and cooked fish, cover, and take off heat to
poach the shrimp and warm through the fish, about 8 to 10 minutes.

TASTE THE SOUP and add salt and pepper if needed. Remove bay leaf. Discard
unopened shellfish. Scoop shellfish and fish in equal portions into serving bowls and
ladle the soup until bowls are full.

IF USING FRESH FISH, season the filets generously with salt. Heat 1 tablespoon
of oil in a non-stick pan. When oil is shimmering, add filets to the pan and sear for
4 minutes. Carefully flip to second side for another minute and remove pan
from heat.

LOBSTER AND CRAB ROLL

Growing up on Long Island as a child and subsequently visiting my mother's house on the North Fork every summer as an adult, exposed me to Northeast favorites like clam rolls and lobster rolls. I remember stopping at Lunch, a well-known eating place on the way to the Hamptons and Montauk, where they specialize in lobster rolls. Whenever I have lobster, if there is any leftover meat, I'll sauté it in butter and add it to scrambled eggs or make a lobster salad. One evening there were two claws left over, not really enough for a salad. I opened a can of crabmeat and made a lobster and crab salad and served it in a hotdog bun. Amazingly good!

Serves 4

1 lobster tail, out of shell and
    cut into 1-inch chunks
2 lobster claws, out of shell
    and cut into 1-inch chunks
½ pound crabmeat (claw,
    jumbo, lump, or colossal)
¼ cup celery, finely diced
2 tablespoons crème fraîche
    (or plain yogurt)
2 tablespoons mayonnaise
1 tablespoon fresh tarragon,
    finely chopped
1 tablespoon fresh chives,
    finely chopped
½ lemon, juiced
Salt and pepper to taste
4 hotdog buns
1 tablespoon butter, melted

COMBINE ALL INGREDIENTS in a medium-sized bowl. Brush melted butter on the inside of lightly toasted hotdog buns and spoon salad equally into them.

MIXED SEAFOOD CEVICHE

The easiest and most delicious way to use up excess fish is ceviche. The acidity of the limes literally "cooks" the fish. At Epicure, we make two different types of ceviche: seafood and shrimp. The seafood ceviche recipe depends on what fish we have available. This recipe is quite versatile in the types of fish you can use and the added accompaniments. If you don't have fresh peppers, roasted red peppers work just as well.

Makes 1½ quarts

2 pounds mixed seafood
    (salmon, grouper, tilapia,
    snapper, swordfish,
    calamari, shrimp)
12 ounces fresh lime juice
    (about 12 limes)
¼ red onion, diced
½ orange bell pepper,
    deseeded and thinly sliced
1 tablespoon fresh cilantro,
    finely chopped
1 tablespoon fresh parsley,
    finely chopped
½ jalapeño, deseeded and
    minced
½ teaspoon dried oregano
½ teaspoon dried basil
½ teaspoon chili paste
½ teaspoon wasabi powder
    (optional)
½ teaspoon sugar
½ teaspoon white pepper

POUR FRESH LIME JUICE into a plastic container. Add fish and let sit at room temperature for 10 minutes while you prep the vegetables. Using a slotted spoon, transfer the fish to a large mixing bowl with 1 cup of the liquid. Add the rest of the ingredients and mix well. Taste for salt and sugar. Refrigerate for at least 1 hour before serving.

CHAPTER 11: FROM THE LAND

Poultry and Meat Entrées

CHICKEN MEATLOAF
with Roasted Vegetables

My grandmother used to make a meatloaf with a hard-boiled egg in the middle, which always made us kids laugh. Harvey Katz, Epicure's meat manager from the 1970s and '80s (and still working today "behind the butcher block") claims to have invented "chickenloaf." One might say that my "salvage chef" moniker was created the day Rudi and Harvey asked me to do something special with 40 pounds of excess chicken trim. The result was my County Style Chicken Meatloaf. This recipe uses roasted veggies to keep it super moist, a hint of smokiness from the paprika, and a Harissa glaze for a deep red crust.

Serves 8

GLAZE
½ cup ketchup
½ cup Harissa

MEATLOAF
1 bell pepper (red, yellow or orange), diced
1 zucchini, diced
1 yellow squash, diced
½ red onion, diced
2 garlic cloves, minced
2 tablespoons olive oil
2 teaspoons salt
3 pounds ground chicken or turkey
½ cup panko breadcrumbs (or plain breadcrumbs)
1 egg
1 cup ketchup
1 tablespoon Dijon mustard
1 tablespoon Worcestershire sauce
2 teaspoons smoked paprika
2 teaspoons salt
1 teaspoon dried basil
1 teaspoon dried oregano

PREHEAT OVEN TO 375°F.

PLACE VEGETABLES IN A ROASTING PAN, drizzle with oil, sprinkle with salt, toss to combine, and roast until slightly brown, about 14 minutes. Remove from oven and allow vegetables to cool, about 10 minutes.

COMBINE KETCHUP AND HARISSA in a small bowl. Set aside.

IN A LARGE MIXING BOWL, add ground chicken, roasted vegetables, the remaining ingredients, and mix with hands until completely blended. Form into 1 loaf or 2 smaller loaves. Place on a baking sheet lined with parchment paper. Brush glaze on entire surface of meatloaf and place in the oven for 40 minutes. Turn the baking sheet 180° after 20 minutes.

The best meat and chicken dishes are the ones made from scratch, using fresh ingredients, perfectly seasoned vegetables, and lots of fresh herbs. Stews and slow cooked dishes transform fairly inexpensive cuts of meat into incredibly tender and flavorful comfort food. These dishes freeze well and can be used to create salvage meals later on.

Leftover cooked meats can be made into new stews, rice dishes, and many other salvage meals, which become cost effective and flavorful when incorporated with your few-days-old vegetables. Probably the best aspect of salvaging cooked pieces of beef and chicken is that, unlike traditional slow cooking methods that take hours, these dishes can be made in minutes, as the cooked meats are added at the end of the cooking process.

PULLED CHICKEN WITH BBQ SAUCE

A low and slow cooking method is typically used for tough cuts of meat to tenderize them and, in some preparations, so they can be easily "pulled." Since leftover chicken is already cooked and has given up most of its juices and flavor when it was first enjoyed, I created a recipe to "pull" the chicken into pieces and combine them with a savory and sweet BBQ sauce. My son, Miles, will eat two of these sandwiches and ask for extra sauce. These have huge flavor and take just minutes to prepare. Enjoy on a bun, over rice, or with a side vegetable.

Serves 2

2 cooked chicken breasts
¾ cup *Michael's Smoky Single Malt BBQ Sauce* (page 51)
4 hamburger buns

"PULL" THE CHICKEN BREAST PIECES INTO A BOWL. Add BBQ sauce and mix to coat evenly. Place a generous pile of chicken on each bun bottom and top with other half to complete sandwich.

Creative uses . . .
- *Serve over reheated cooked rice with a spoon of sour cream.*
- *Swirl in plain yogurt and serve in a taco shell or tortilla with your favorite shredded cheese.*
- *Add cooked leftover vegetables to the chicken and enjoy as a main course.*

CRISPY LIME CHICKEN IN LETTUCE CUPS

Serves 4

2 tablespoon olive oil
¾ pound cooked chicken,
    finely chopped (small
    pebble-sized pieces)
Salt and pepper
½ teaspoon red chili flake
1 teaspoon fresh ginger,
    peeled and minced (or ½
    teaspoon ground ginger)
1 lime, juiced
1 shallot, sliced
1 teaspoon granulated sugar
½ teaspoon ground
    coriander
1 jalapeño, seeded and
    minced
2 tablespoons soy sauce
2 teaspoons fish sauce
1 teaspoon rice vinegar
1 teaspoon light brown sugar
2 tablespoons sesame oil
1 tablespoon canola oil
8 lettuce cups (iceberg, bibb)
2 limes, cut into quarters

ADD 1 TABLESPOON OF OIL to a large pan over medium-high heat. When oil is shimmering, add chopped chicken, salt, and pepper to taste. Stirring frequently, brown the chicken bits, about 6 minutes. Add chili flake, ginger, 1 tablespoon of the lime juice, and stir for 1 minute to combine. Take off heat and scrape chicken bits into a bowl.

WIPE OUT THE PAN with a sheet of paper towel, and heat 1 tablespoon of oil over medium heat. Add shallots, sugar, and coriander. Stir frequently so that shallots don't burn. Cook for 2 to 3 minutes to caramelize the shallots. Add in the chicken and mix to combine the ingredients.

TO MAKE THE SAUCE, whisk all the remaining ingredients together except for the 2 oils. When ingredients are well blended, slowly drizzle the oils while whisking. Scoop chicken mixture into lettuce cups and drizzle with sauce. Serve with a squeeze of fresh lime.

One of our favorite quickly-prepared dinners at home is a Thai-inspired crispy and spicy beef in lettuce cups. To cut down on the fat content, I decided to try it with cooked chicken. Try this recipe with beef, pork, duck, or turkey.

MOROCCAN CHICKEN STEW

A great way to use up leftover meats and poultry is with a savory stew. Typically stews take hours to cook to break down the tough cuts of meat. Using cooked meat (or in this case, chicken), literally takes no more than 30 minutes. This version incorporates some salvage ingredients from the pantry including raisins, canned tomatoes, beans, and left-over cooked rice. The addition of my steak sauce at the end livens up the stew and gives it a terrific tangy flavor. Use vegetables you have on hand as well as your favorite herbs and spices to create your own scrumptious salvage stew!

Serves 4

2 tablespoons olive oil
1 onion, diced
2 garlic cloves, peeled and
   rough chopped
1 bell pepper, seeded and
   sliced
2 sprigs fresh oregano, finely
   chopped (leaves only), or
   1 teaspoon dried oregano
1 tablespoon *Savory Spice
   Blend* (page 32)
1 tablespoon tomato paste
1 cup white wine
1 (14-ounce) can whole
   tomatoes
1 (14-ounce) can beans
   (kidney, pinto, or whatever
   you have in your pantry),
   drained

IN A MEDIUM-SIZED POT, heat oil over a medium-high heat. Add onions and garlic and cook to soften, about 5 minutes. Stir frequently so they don't brown.

ADD PEPPERS, OREGANO, SPICE BLEND, and tomato paste and stir to combine. Continue cooking for an additional 2 minutes to soften the peppers and release the flavors of the spices. Add wine, lower the heat, and reduce the liquid by half. Add bay leaf and stir in tomatoes and beans. Simmer for 20 minutes to thicken. Stir occasionally to prevent sticking to the bottom of the pot.

WHEN STEW HAS THICKENED, remove the bay leaf, fold in the cooked chicken, raisins, and steak sauce and continue simmering for 2 to 3 minutes. Once chicken is warmed through, taste for seasoning and add salt if needed. Swirl in the yogurt and serve immediately over rice.

1 bay leaf
2 pounds cooked boneless
   or bone-in chicken
   (breasts, thighs, legs, or
   assorted)
½ cup golden raisins
1 tablespoon *Steak Sauce*
   (page 57)
Salt and pepper
1 cup plain yogurt or sour
   cream (optional)
2 cups of cooked rice (see
   page 163 for reheating)

Creative uses . . .

- *For the vegetarian, this stew can be made without chicken. Simply add cut up vegetables with the onion and garlic.*
- *If you have roasted tomatoes on hand (page 54), substitute for canned tomatoes and prepare stew simply with white beans, 1 teaspoon of your favorite spice, and a cup of white wine.*
- *One of my favorite versions is a Spanish-style stew made by adding chorizo in with the onions and cooked leftover potatoes (boiled or roasted) instead of the beans. Leave out the raisins and serve with shredded Manchego cheese.*

CHICKEN FRIED RICE

One of the most thrown away items in the refrigerator is cooked rice from a Chinese take-out dinner. If reheated properly, cooked rice makes a great partner with vegetables, meat, chicken, and seafood. This delicious fried rice recipe can be made with shrimp or beef and takes no more than 10 minutes. The ingredients and the simple cooking method bring out all the flavors with just a touch of soy sauce, but feel free to add oyster sauce, fish sauce, or other seasonings of your choosing.

Serves 4

3 tablespoons canola oil (or vegetable or peanut)
1 shallot, sliced
1 teaspoon fresh ginger, peeled and minced (or ½ teaspoon ground ginger)
1 baby bok choy, cut into ¼-inch strips (about 1 cup)
1 teaspoon ground coriander
2 eggs
2 cups cooked rice
1 cooked chicken breast, sliced into ½-inch strips
¼ cup peas (frozen or fresh)
½ cup iceberg lettuce, sliced into thin strips
2 tablespoons soy sauce
1 teaspoon fish sauce (optional)

IN A NON-STICK PAN, heat 1 tablespoon of oil over medium-high heat. When oil is shimmering, add shallots, ginger, coriander, and a small pinch of salt. Cook for 1 minute, stirring constantly. Add the bok choy and cook until vegetables are soft, about 5 minutes. Remove vegetables to a bowl and set aside.

WIPE OUT THE PAN with a sheet of paper towel, add 1 tablespoon of oil, and place pan over medium heat. When oil is shimmering, crack eggs into the pan and stir with a wooden spoon. Let eggs set for about 10 seconds and then fold in the rice. Mix together and separate any clumps of rice with the back of the spoon.

ADD THE COOKED VEGETABLES, chicken, peas, lettuce, soy sauce (and fish sauce if using) and mix to combine until chicken is heated through, about 2 minutes. Serve immediately with some extra soy sauce.

WINTER BEAN BEEF STEW

Similar to the Moroccan Chicken Stew (page 196), a stew using cooked beef versus fresh reduces the cooking time by hours as well as using up perfectly edible food you have in your refrigerator. This stew is versatile because you can use any vegetables you have, any flavored stock from your freezer (or canned), just about any cut of meat (either cooked or fresh), any beans in your pantry, and you can replace any herbs or spices with your favorites . . . but try my recipe first. This is the ultimate comfort food over buttered noodles.

Serves 4 to 6

2 tablespoons olive oil
1 onion, diced
2 garlic cloves, peeled and smashed
2 carrots, peeled and sliced on the bias
2 celery stalks, sliced on the bias
2 parsnips, peeled and sliced on the bias (optional)
3 sprigs rosemary
3 sprigs thyme
2 cups red wine
1 tablespoon flour
2 cups beef stock (chicken or vegetable)
1 (14-ounce) can beans, drained (white, red)
2 bay leaves
2 teaspoons smoked paprika
1 teaspoon ground cumin
Salt and pepper
1 potato, peeled and diced
2 pounds cooked beef, cut into 2-inch cubes (pork, chicken, or turkey)
1 tablespoon red wine vinegar

IN A MEDIUM-SIZED POT, heat oil over a medium-high heat. Add onions and garlic and cook to soften, about 5 minutes. Stir frequently so they don't brown.

ADD CARROTS, CELERY, PARSNIPS, and herbs and stir to combine. Continue cooking to soften vegetables, about 5 minutes. Add wine, lower the heat, and reduce the liquid by half. Add stock, beans, bay leaves, paprika, and cumin. Simmer for 20 minutes to thicken.

WHEN STEW HAS THICKENED, remove the bay leaves, add the potatoes, and continue cooking for 8 minutes until potatoes are fork tender. Fold in the cooked beef and continue simmering for 2 to 3 minutes. Once beef is warmed through, taste for seasoning and add salt if needed. Add vinegar, give the stew a final stir, and serve immediately over rice or buttered noodles.

BIG BOLD BEEF AND ITALIAN SAUSAGE CHILI

Serves 4 to 6

½ pound cooked ground beef
½ pound cooked Italian sausage
½ pound beef chuck flats, cubed ¾-inch
2 onions, chopped
4 garlic, minced
2 red bell peppers, seeded and diced
1 poblano (or cubanelle or jalapeño) pepper, seeded and diced
¼ cup *Chili Spice Blend* (page 31)
1 (12-ounce) can beer
1 (14-ounce) can whole tomatoes
2 cups stock (chicken or beef)
2 tablespoons tomato paste
1 (14-ounce) can beans, drained (white or red)

IF USING UNCOOKED MEATS, brown ground beef and ground sausage in a large non-stick skillet. Remove the cooked meat and drain all the fat. Next, brown the cubed chuck (add a little olive oil if the meat sticks). Cook meat until browned. Remove and drain all the fat. Set aside.

IF USING COOKED MEATS, add 1 tablespoon of oil to a large heavy-bottomed pot and place over medium-high heat. When oil is shimmering, add onions and garlic and cook to soften, about 5 minutes. Add all the peppers, spice blend, and mix together. Cook for 2 to 3 minutes to toast the spices and soften the peppers.

ADD BEER TO DEGLAZE THE BOTTOM. Scrape the bottom of pot with a wooden spoon to loosen any stuck vegetables. Add all the cooked meat, tomatoes, stock, and tomato paste. Mix well and bring to a boil. Add beans, lower the heat, and simmer for 40 minutes, stirring frequently to keep the bottom from burning.

Adjust seasoning and add smoked paprika for more smokiness.

This is one of Epicure's biggest sellers and my favorite Sunday meal during football season. You can make this from scratch (using fresh meats) or use cooked leftover meats. Cooked ground beef and sausage freeze really well in an airtight container or freezer bag, so I always have both on hand. I love to combine different cuts of meat in my chili, and for this recipe I've incorporated ground beef, chunks of sausage out of the casing, and beef chuck cut into 1-inch cubes. For spicier chili, add ¼ to ½ teaspoon of cayenne pepper to the spice blend or add your favorite hot sauce at the end.

SPICY BEEF TACOS

What better way to cook with your family than organizing a Taco Night? Tacos are a great way to reuse ground beef, vegetables, shredded cheese, and the last of the sour cream. If you don't have taco shells, you can use pita bread warmed in the oven. This recipe uses leftover hamburgers and a quick blender Pico de Gallo, but you can also make from scratch with fresh ground beef and use your favorite salsa or hot sauce.

Serves 4

4 cooked hamburgers
1 tablespoon *Chili Spice Blend* (page 31)
½ lime, juiced
1 cup lettuce, shredded
1 cup chopped tomatoes
1 cup cheddar cheese, shredded
1 cup sour cream or yogurt
4 taco shells

IN A MEDIUM-SIZED SKILLET heat 1 tablespoon of oil. Crumble hamburgers in pan and add spice blend and lime juice. Continue cooking until meat is heated through. Break apart any clumps with the back of a wooden spoon.

PICO DE GALLO
1 (14-ounce) can diced tomatoes
¼ cup red onion, diced
½ bell pepper, seeded and rough chopped
1 jalapeño, deseeded and minced
1 lime, juiced and zested
2 teaspoons salt

PLACE ALL INGREDIENTS in a blender and pulse several times to combine. Leave it chunky.

TO SERVE, fill taco shells with meat and top with Pico de Gallo, followed by your favorite toppings. Another tasty option is to combine the salsa with the meat mixture and spoon into the taco shells or warmed pita bread.

BEEF STIR-FRY

For a quick, delicious, and healthy meal using leftover beef, chicken, pork, or shellfish, try making a stir-fry. All you need is a hot pan, hot oil, fresh or leftover vegetables and meat, and a drizzle of soy sauce.

Serves 4

1 tablespoon canola oil (vegetable, peanut, safflower)
½ red onion
2 bell peppers (one red, one green), seeded and cut into ¼-inch slices
1 zucchini, cut into ¼-inch sticks (about 3 inches long)
1 teaspoon minced garlic
2 teaspoons soy sauce
1 pound cooked or fresh meat (steak cut into ½-inch strips)
1 teaspoon oyster sauce
Black pepper

HEAT 1 TABLESPOON OF OIL in a pan over a high heat. When oil is shimmering, add onions, peppers, and zucchini with a small pinch of salt. Shake the pan frequently as you coat the vegetables with oil and quickly sear them. Once the vegetables are slightly brown and have begun to soften, add the garlic, cooked meat, soy sauce, and oyster sauce. Toss to combine for about 1 minute, until the meat is warmed through. Serve immediately with rice, soy sauce, and some fresh cut limes.

ITALIAN MEATLOAF

I like to make meatloaf the same way I make my meatballs: milk-soaked bread, sautéed onions and garlic, fresh herbs, and usually Pecorino Romano because of its natural saltiness. This recipe came about when we had about three dozen too many Italian meatballs in the fresh meat case at Epicure. I mixed them all together with fresh herbs, eggs to make them moist, and a slice of mozzarella on top.

Serves 2

2 slices white bread, crusts
    cut off and torn into 1-inch
    pieces
½ cup milk
1 tablespoon olive oil
1 onion, diced
2 garlic cloves, minced
1 egg
¼ cup Pecorino Romano (or
    Parmesan)
2 tablespoons chopped
    parsley
3 to 4 basil leaves, finely
    chopped
1 pound ground meat (beef,
    veal, pork)
4 ounces fresh mozzarella,
    cut into ¼-inch slices
1 cup *The Best Basic Tomato
    Sauce* (page 54)

PREHEAT OVEN TO 400°F.

HEAT 1 TABLESPOON OF OIL in a large pot over medium heat. Add the onion and garlic, and cook for 6 to 8 minutes until the vegetables are soft and translucent. If vegetables begin to brown, lower the heat. Once the vegetables are cooked, take the pot off the heat and let cool.

PLACE BREAD PIECES IN A SMALL BOWL. Pour enough milk over the bread to moisten and let it soak while the onions are cooling.

COMBINE THE MEATS (if using more than one) in a large bowl. Add egg, cheese, parsley, and basil and season generously with salt and pepper (about 1 teaspoon each). Use your hands to squeeze the excess milk out of the bread and add to the meat mixture along with the cooled cooked vegetables. Gently combine all the ingredients with your hands or with a fork until just mixed together. Don't overwork or the meatloaf will be tough. Divide into 2 and with wet hands, shape them into oval-shaped loaves.

PLACE LOAVES IN NON-STICK MINI LOAF PANS (6 by 3-inch) or in a baking pan and bake for 15 minutes. Remove from oven and place cheese slices on top of loaves. Return to oven for 2 to 3 minutes to melt cheese. Garnish with fresh basil.

CHAPTER 12: BUTTA LA PASTA

Pasta Entrées

ANGEL HAIR WITH TOMATOES,
Mozzarella, and Basil

Simple, five ingredients, 10 minutes. Delicious. A great way to use up tomatoes and wilting basil.

Serves 4

2 tablespoons olive oil
2 garlic cloves, minced
3 Roma tomatoes (or 1 large tomato), deseeded and diced
1 pound angel hair pasta
½ pound mozzarella, torn into ½-inch pieces
½ bunch fresh basil, finely chopped
Salt and black pepper

IN A LARGE SAUTÉ PAN, heat olive oil over medium-high heat. When oil is shimmering, add garlic and cook for 15 seconds. Shake the pan so that it doesn't burn. Add diced tomatoes and cook for 3 minutes to soften.

COOK THE PASTA for just under 2 minutes until al dente (check pasta package for cooking times) or refresh leftover pasta by dropping in boiling water for 15 to 20 seconds. Drain the pasta and do not rinse.

ADD PASTA to sautéed tomatoes, followed by the mozzarella and basil. Toss in the pan and continue to cook until cheese begins to melt and entire contents are warmed through, about 1 minute. Season generously with salt and pepper. Serve immediately with a healthy drizzle of olive oil on top of each portion and garnish with fresh basil leaves.

I love pasta. Fresh, hot, cold, baked, even leftover pasta warmed in the microwave. You can quickly refresh un-sauced cooked pasta by dropping it in boiling water for 15 to 20 seconds. Pasta with sauce can be easily reheated, but is best when livened up with some new ingredients, a handful of cheese for instance, and baked for 10 minutes. My pasta creations typically utilize three ingredients—a combination of salvage and fresh. They can be made with fresh pasta, but when you don't have the time or have a bowl or two of leftover pasta in your refrigerator, try these combinations and be inspired to create your own with the ingredients you have on hand.

CREAMY ORECCHIETTE PASTA
with Prosciutto and Asparagus

½ pound asparagus, cut into 2-inch pieces (tips and stalks)
Salt
2 tablespoons olive oil
½ cup prosciutto (can substitute bacon, pancetta, or ham), rough chopped
½ cup light cream (mascarpone or ricotta)
1 pound orecchiette
¼ cup Parmesan cheese, grated
1 teaspoon *All Purpose Spice Blend* (page 29)

IN A LARGE SAUTÉ PAN, heat olive oil over medium-high heat. When oil is shimmering, add prosciutto and cook for 2 to 3 minutes.

DROP ASPARAGUS PIECES INTO SALTED BOILING WATER for 40 seconds. Immediately drain and add to prosciutto. Stir in light cream, lower heat, and continue cooking for 1 minute to thicken.

COOK THE PASTA for 8 minutes until al dente (check pasta package for cooking times), or refresh leftover pasta by dropping in boiling water for 15 to 20 seconds. Drain the pasta and do not rinse.

ADD PASTA TO PROSCIUTTO MIXTURE. Toss in the pan to blend ingredients. Taste for seasoning. Add grated cheese, give another quick toss, and serve immediately with a healthy drizzle of olive oil on top of each portion.

I love this "ear" pasta. It holds the sauce like no other pasta shape. Substitute any vegetable for the asparagus and bacon or leftover ham for the prosciutto.

Serves 4

FARFALLE PASTA WITH GRILLED CHICKEN, Spinach, and Mushrooms

Chicken, spinach, and mushrooms are a fabulous trio and I always seem to have them leftover in my refrigerator. Use cooked chicken, arugula if you have it, onions or scallions if you don't have shallots, and any mushrooms. I also love to add crispy bacon.

Serves 4

2 tablespoons olive oil
1 cup mushrooms, sliced
1 shallot, thinly sliced
2 cups baby spinach, stems trimmed
¾ pound grilled chicken
1 pound farfalle (bowtie pasta)
¼ cup Parmesan cheese, grated
Salt and pepper

IN A LARGE SAUTÉ PAN, heat olive oil over medium-high heat. When oil is shimmering, add mushrooms in one layer. Sprinkle with salt and pepper and brown without moving them around, about 2 minutes. Using tongs, turn mushrooms over and add more oil if pan is dry. After cooking untouched for 1 minute, add shallots and shake pan to toss vegetables together. Add freshly rinsed spinach and gently turn in the pan to coat with oil and wilt, 1 minute. Add chicken and toss to combine.

COOK THE PASTA for 7 to 8 minutes until al dente (check pasta package for cooking times) or refresh leftover pasta by dropping in boiling water for 15 to 20 seconds. Drain the pasta and do not rinse.

ADD PASTA TO MUSHROOM and spinach mixture. Toss in the pan to blend ingredients. Taste for seasoning. Add grated cheese, give another quick toss, and serve immediately with a healthy drizzle of olive oil.

FETTUCCINI WITH ROASTED
Portabella, Turkey Bacon, Pecorino Romano

This is a great pasta dish for those people who don't eat red meat but enjoy a hearty, satisfying, comfort-food meal. The portabellas are a perfect substitute for meat and the turkey bacon lends its smokiness.

Serves 4

6 strips turkey bacon
2 tablespoons olive oil
2 portabella mushrooms, cut into ½-inch slices
2 garlic cloves, minced
Salt
1 pound fettuccini
½ cup mascarpone cheese (ricotta or light cream)
¼ cup Pecorino Romano (or Parmesan)
Salt and black pepper

PREHEAT OVEN TO 400°F.

LAY BACON STRIPS IN A BAKING PAN and place in the oven for 12 minutes, until crispy. Remove from oven and, once cooled, break into 2-inch pieces. Place in a large mixing bowl.

TOSS TOGETHER MUSHROOMS, oil, garlic, and salt in a bowl. Transfer to a baking pan and roast in the oven for 8 to 10 minutes. Remove from oven and add mushrooms to the bacon.

COOK THE PASTA for 8 minutes until al dente (check pasta package for cooking times) or refresh leftover pasta by dropping in boiling water for 15 to 20 seconds. Drain the pasta and do not rinse.

ADD PASTA TO BOWL with mushrooms and bacon and stir in mascarpone. Sprinkle grated cheese and taste for seasoning. Serve immediately with a healthy drizzle of olive oil.

PENNE WITH ROASTED RED PEPPERS,
Capers, Artichoke Hearts, and Feta

Serves 4

2 tablespoons olive oil
1 large roasted red pepper, sliced
1 tablespoon capers
8 artichoke hearts, cut in quarters (about 1 cup)
½ cup feta cheese, crumbled
1 pound penne
¼ cup Parmesan cheese, grated
Salt and pepper

IN A LARGE SAUTÉ PAN, heat olive oil over medium-high heat. When oil is shimmering, add red pepper, capers, and artichoke hearts. Sauté for 2 minutes.

COOK THE PASTA for 7 to 8 minutes until al dente (check pasta package for cooking times) or refresh leftover pasta by dropping in boiling water for 15 to 20 seconds. Drain the pasta and do not rinse.

ADD PASTA TO PAN AND TOSS TO BLEND INGREDIENTS. Taste for seasoning. Add feta, give another quick toss and serve immediately with a healthy drizzle of olive oil.

PENNE WITH ROASTED BUTTERNUT SQUASH
Swiss Chard, and Sausage

Serves 4

2 tablespoons olive oil
½ butternut squash, peeled, halved lengthwise, deseeded and cut into 1-inch chunks
Salt and black pepper
½ pound cooked ground sausage (ground beef, chicken, turkey)
1 large bunch Swiss chard, coarsely chopped
¼ cup stock (vegetable or chicken)
1 pound penne

PREHEAT OVEN TO 400°F.

TOSS TOGETHER SQUASH CHUNKS, salt, and pepper in a bowl. Transfer to a baking pan and roast in the oven for 15 minutes. Remove from oven and set aside.

IN A LARGE SAUTÉ PAN over medium-high heat, add cooked sausage and warm through, about 2 minutes. Add chard and stock to the pan and gently turn with tongs to combine and wilt.

COOK THE PASTA for 8 minutes until al dente (check pasta package for cooking times) or refresh leftover pasta by dropping in boiling water for 15 to 20 seconds. Drain the pasta and do not rinse.

ADD PASTA TO PAN and toss to combine. Taste for seasoning. Serve immediately with a healthy drizzle of olive oil.

SPAGHETTI WITH ROASTED GARLIC,
Lemon Zest, and Brussels Sprouts

This pasta dish is one of my favorite dishes when I want to impress but need to keep the cost and prep time down. The four main ingredients are usually in my kitchen and I can toss it together with leftover refreshed spaghetti in less than 40 minutes.

Serves 4

4 tablespoons olive oil
1 head of garlic, sliced in half, crosswise (exposing the cloves)
½ pound Brussels sprouts, ends cut off and halved
½ cup panko breadcrumbs, lightly toasted (in a dry pan over medium heat or in the oven for 2 minutes at 350°F.)
1 pound spaghetti
1 lemon, zested and juiced
¼ cup Parmesan cheese, grated
1 teaspoon *Savory Spice Blend* (page 32)

PREHEAT OVEN TO 400°F.

PLACE GARLIC HEAD HALVES onto a piece of 8 by 8-inch square of foil, drizzle with 1 tablespoon of olive oil, sprinkle with salt and pepper, and then bring the ends of the foil together forming a pouch. Place pouch in the oven for 30 minutes.

TOSS BRUSSELS SPROUTS with 2 tablespoons of olive oil, salt, and pepper in a bowl. Transfer to a baking pan and roast in the oven for 15 minutes (place in the oven when garlic is halfway roasted). Remove both garlic and Brussels sprouts from oven and set aside.

COOK THE PASTA for 8 minutes until al dente (check pasta package for cooking times) or refresh leftover pasta by dropping in boiling water for 15 to 20 seconds. Drain the pasta and do not rinse.

PLACE PASTA INTO A LARGE BOWL, drizzle with 1 tablespoon of olive oil, the juice of the lemon, and toss. Open foil pouch and squeeze cloves out of garlic head. Add garlic and Brussels sprouts to the bowl of pasta.

ADD GRATED CHEESE AND SPICE BLEND to the pasta and toss to combine. Top with lemon zest and toasted panko, a drizzle of olive oil, and serve.

BACON, TRUFFLE, 4-CHEESE MAC 'N' CHEESE

This dish is absolutely the kids' favorite for dinner. I always keep my cheese sauce in the freezer so I can whip up a mac 'n' cheese in no time. Simply defrost the sauce in the microwave and add to pasta. If you don't have truffle oil, you can add leftover cooked mushrooms.

Serves 4

3 slices bacon
½ pound macaroni
1½ teaspoons truffle oil
3 cups *Gruyère, Cheddar, and Bleu Cheese Sauce* (page 52)
2 teaspoons dried parsley
Salt
¼ cup Gruyère cheese, shredded
¼ cup sharp cheddar cheese, shredded
2 tablespoons Parmesan cheese, grated

PREHEAT OVEN TO 375°F. Grease 4 (8-ounce) ramekins with butter or use large baking dish.

LAY BACON STRIPS IN A BAKING PAN and place in oven for 15 minutes. Remove from oven and place on a folded paper towel to absorb grease. Once bacon is cooled, break into pieces.

COOK MACARONI in salted boiling water and drain. Return to pot and toss with 1 teaspoon of truffle oil to keep from sticking. Set aside.

IN A LARGE NON-STICK SKILLET, warm the cheese sauce over medium heat. Or, if using frozen sauce, defrost in microwave until smooth but not bubbling. Pour sauce over macaroni and add bacon, parsley, and remaining ½ teaspoon of truffle oil. Stir to combine and taste for seasoning.

FILL RAMEKINS JUST BELOW THE RIM with macaroni mixture and top with cheeses (combine cheeses together before topping). Bake for 25 minutes until cheese is bubbly and brown.

Only one aspect of a course should be the star, and these "salvage" salads and side dishes can readily take center stage with a simply prepared protein.

CHAPTER 13: ON THE SIDE

Salads and Vegetable Side Dishes

8 VEGETABLE KALE AND BEET SALAD
with Thyme Curry Vinaigrette

SALAD

2 beets (red or golden),
  peeled and quartered
2 carrots, peeled and cut on
  the bias into 1-inch pieces
1 cucumber, halved
  horizontally, deseeded and
  diced
1 cup green cabbage,
  shredded
2 celery stalks, diced
½ cup red onion, diced
2 scallions (white and
  light green parts), finely
  chopped
1 bunch kale, ribs removed
  and chopped

DRESSING

1 shallot, minced
1 garlic clove, minced
3 sprigs fresh thyme (leaves
  only), finely chopped
½ cup orange juice
¼ cup cider vinegar
2 teaspoons curry powder
1 teaspoon dried thyme
½ cup canola oil (or olive oil,
  grapeseed, vegetable)
Salt

PREHEAT OVEN TO 375°F.

PLACE BEETS AND CARROTS in a small roasting pan with a drizzle of olive oil and a sprinkle of salt. Add 2 tablespoons of water and cover tightly with foil. Place in the oven for 15 minutes to steam. Remove from the oven, take off the foil, and set aside to cool. (If you don't want your carrots to have a purple tint from the beets, roast them separately.)

TOSS THE COOLED BEETS AND CARROTS with all the other salad ingredients in a large salad bowl. Make the dressing by combining all ingredients in a separate bowl, except for the oil. Slowly whisk in the oil to emulsify. Taste for seasoning. Pour dressing generously over the salad and toss.

The inspiration behind this salad is my 8 Vegetable Purée Soup combined with the increasingly popular kale. Not only is kale super healthy and delicious, but it holds up to just about any dressing. Don't worry if you don't have all eight vegetables . . . use what you have.

Serves 4

SPICY SHRIMP, CUCUMBER,
and Tomato Salad with Crumbled Feta

I love this quick, refreshing salad that helps use up a few leftover cooked shrimp, tomato, and cucumber, and the last bit of crumbly cheese (feta, bleu, gorgonzola).

Serves 2

½ teaspoon smoked paprika
½ teaspoon ground cumin
½ teaspoon salt
¼ teaspoon cayenne pepper
2 tablespoon olive oil
6 cooked shrimp (grilled,
   broiled, pan fried)*
½ cucumber (seedless), cut
   into 1-inch pieces
2 tomatoes, quartered
2 ounces feta cheese,
   crumbled
dash of fish sauce
1 teaspoon fresh cilantro,
   chopped (or parsley)

PLACE COOKED SHRIMP IN A BOWL and add the spices plus 1 tablespoon of the oil. Toss to coat the shrimp evenly. Add cucumber, tomatoes, feta, fish sauce, cilantro, and remaining tablespoon of olive oil. Toss again to combine. Serve in a martini glass for dramatic effect.

IF USING RAW SHRIMP, coat the shrimp in the spices and oil and then transfer to a hot pan. Sauté quickly for 2 minutes until shrimp are just about cooked through. Remove from heat and place in refrigerator for 20 minutes to cool.

ARUGULA AND HEARTS OF PALM
Salad with Orange Vinaigrette

This salad has become a weekly feature at Epicure and uses up ingredients from several sections of the market.

Serves 4

SALAD

8 cups arugula

1 (14-ounce) can hearts of palm, drained and cut crosswise into ½-inch slices

1 cup tomatoes (cherry, grape), halved

½ cup dates, pitted and cut in half, lengthwise

½ cup whole smoked almonds (walnuts, pecans), plus 2 tablespoons for garnish

½ cup gorgonzola cheese, crumbled, plus 2 tablespoons for garnish

DRESSING

4 ounces orange juice

2 ounces cider vinegar

1 tablespoon soy sauce

1 teaspoon Dijon mustard

1 teaspoon dried thyme

½ cup olive oil

Salt

TOSS THE SALAD INGREDIENTS in a large salad bowl. Make the dressing by combining all ingredients except for the oil in a separate bowl. Slowly whisk in the oil to emulsify. Taste for seasoning. Pour dressing generously over the salad and toss. Garnish with almonds and cheese.

ROMAINE, PEAR, AND FETA SALAD
with Strawberry Vinaigrette

Whenever you have berries left over, purée them and add to your salad dressings for deep color and a sweet note. Try this dressing over vanilla and strawberry ice cream!

Serves 4

1 head romaine, chopped
2 pears, halved, cored, and
   cut into 1-inch chunks
½ cup pine nuts
½ cup dried cranberries
   (or raisins)
½ cup feta, crumbled

DRESSING

1 cup strawberries
   (or blueberry, blackberry,
   raspberry)
1 teaspoon sugar
1 lemon, zested and juiced
2 tablespoons balsamic
   vinegar
½ teaspoon dried basil
½ teaspoon dried tarragon
½ cup olive oil
Salt

PLACE PINE NUTS IN A DRY PAN over medium-low heat and shake pan back and forth. Don't leave the pan unattended as the pine nuts will burn easily. Continue to shake the pan until you see the pine nuts begin to toast, about 1 to 2 minutes. Remove immediately from the pan and set aside.

TOSS THE SALAD INGREDIENTS in a large salad bowl. Make the dressing by combining all ingredients except for the oil in a mini food processor or blender. Pulse a few times to combine ingredients and then leave it on high while slowly pouring in the oil to emulsify. Taste for seasoning. Pour dressing generously over the salad and toss.

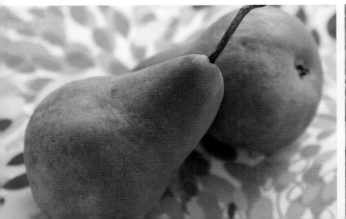

CLASSIC CAESAR
with Smoky Sourdough Croutons

CROUTONS

1 sourdough baguette
(French bread)
2 tablespoons olive oil
1 tablespoon *Spanish Spice
Blend* (page 35)
Salt and black pepper
2 tablespoons Parmesan
cheese, grated

SALAD

1 head romaine, trim off
the root end and keep
whole leaves intact (or if
preferred, rough chop)

DRESSING

2 garlic cloves, smashed,
peeled, and chopped
2 anchovies
½ lemon, juiced
2 egg yolks
1 tablespoon water
1 teaspoon Dijon mustard
¼ cup Parmesan cheese,
grated (plus 1 tablespoon
for finishing)
1 cup olive oil (plus extra for
drizzling)

PREHEAT OVEN TO 400°F.

SMOKY SOURDOUGH CROUTONS

CUT THE BAGUETTE LENGTHWISE IN THIRDS, creating 3 long strips. Then slice crosswise into 1-inch chunks. Place the bread in a medium-sized bowl. Drizzle with 2 tablespoons of olive oil, sprinkle with salt, pepper, and 1 tablespoon of *Spanish Spice Blend*. Toss to combine and pour into a small roasting pan in one layer. Bake until golden brown and crunchy, 4 to 6 minutes, flipping them about halfway through. Remove from oven and immediately sprinkle with grated cheese. Set aside to cool.

DRESSING

In a small food processor or blender, add garlic, anchovies, egg yolks, juice of half a lemon, water, Dijon, and cheese. Pulse a few times to combine ingredients and then leave it on high while slowly pouring in the oil to emulsify. Taste for seasoning.

SALAD

Remove all the excess water from the lettuce leaves by using a salad spinner or blotting with a paper towel. This will allow dressing to coat evenly. Lay the leaves on a platter and spoon the dressing across the stems. Add croutons and sprinkle with Parmesan.

IF USING CHOPPED ROMAINE, simply toss lettuce, croutons, and dressing in a salad bowl and serve with a sprinkling of grated cheese.

The one salad that is my "go to" item on most menus is a Caesar. My son, Miles, requests this salad several nights in a row as long as I agree to make my Caesar dressing and smoky croutons. The dressing can be made in a blender or a small food processor. You can even whisk it together in a bowl. The croutons are smoky and delicious and you can store the extras in an airtight freezer bag.

Serves 4

"BURNT" VEGETABLES—
Cauliflower, Broccoli, Brussels Sprouts, and Green Beans

Thanks to my mom, I love many "burnt" food items. Her trick was to serve the French toast burnt-side down so we wouldn't notice, which of course we always did. Now I order my home fries well done, I like my bagels toasted well and my favorite vegetables are cooked to a deep brown color. Brown these vegetables to your liking but I'm sure you will become a fan of my "burnt" version.

Serves 4
4 cups of mixed vegetables (cauliflower, broccoli, Brussels sprouts, green beans)
Salt
2 tablespoons olive oil
1 tablespoon *Chili Spice Blend* (page 31)
1 lemon, zested

CUT ALL VEGETABLES INTO BITE SIZE PIECES, about 2-inch chunks. Toss all the vegetables in a large pot of salted boiling water for 30 seconds. Remove from the water and drain.

IN A LARGE PAN, heat oil over a high heat. When oil is shimmering and beginning to smoke, add all the blanched vegetables, spice blend, and a good pinch of salt. Toss to combine and then leave for 2 minutes while vegetables brown. Toss again and cook for another 2 minutes. Repeat for a third or fourth time until vegetables are mostly browned. Remove from heat and sprinkle lemon zest over the vegetables. Serve immediately.

ROASTED BROCCOLI WITH SHALLOTS
and Toasted Pine Nuts

We enjoy roasted vegetables more than any other cooking method. Roasted broccoli is probably our favorite side dish and, if there is any leftover, it makes an amazing salvage component. This shake-and-roast method works great with any vegetable . . . cauliflower, green beans, Brussels sprouts, mixed sweet peppers, etc.

Serves 4

1 head broccoli, cut into
   2-inch florets
1 shallot, sliced
¼ cup pine nuts
1 tablespoon sesame seeds
1 tablespoon olive oil
1 teaspoon salt
1 tablespoon Parmesan,
   grated (optional)

PREHEAT OVEN TO 350°F.

PLACE ALL INGREDIENTS in an airtight resealable bag and shake to coat broccoli evenly. Pour into a roasting pan and place in the oven for 15 minutes. Remove from oven, sprinkle with spice blend and grated cheese (optional). Serve immediately.

WHITE BEAN AND SMOKED GOUDA PURÉE

This purée can be made with just about any variety of bean or in combination. Try chickpeas with red kidney beans, or navy beans and pinto beans. Add your favorite spice blend, fresh herbs, and serve with freshly grated cheese you have on hand. This is not only a delicious side dish but works great as a dip served with toasted pita.

Serves 4

1 (15.5 ounce) can white beans
1 cup vegetable or chicken stock
2 sprigs fresh thyme (or ½ teaspoon dried thyme)
2 garlic cloves, smashed and peeled
1 tablespoon olive oil
2 tablespoon Parmesan cheese, grated
½ teaspoon smoked paprika
3 ounces smoked Gouda, shredded, plus 1 tablespoon for garnish
Salt and black pepper

DRAIN THE BEANS and place in a small pot with stock, thyme, and garlic. Bring to a low simmer and then turn off the heat. Cover and let sit for 5 minutes to infuse the beans with the garlic and thyme flavors.

SCOOP OUT THE BEANS AND GARLIC with a slotted spoon and place in a mini food processor. Add 1 tablespoon of the stock, olive oil, Parmesan, and paprika. Purée the mixture until smooth and return to the warm pot. Stir in the Gouda until melted and taste for seasoning. If mixture is too thick, add a little stock to thin it out. Top with shredded cheese and a sprinkle of *Chili Spice Blend* (page 31).

SWEET POTATO AND CELERY ROOT MASH
with Caramelized Shallots and Chive

This side can be made with just sweet potato or a plain baking potato but I love the addition of the celery root. Use red or white onions if you don't have shallots. You can also use leftover cooked potatoes in place of fresh.

Serves 4

1 large sweet potato, peeled and diced (about 1½ cups)
1 celery root, peeled and diced (about 1½ cups)
2 cups vegetable or chicken stock
1 tablespoon olive oil plus 1 teaspoon for finishing
1 shallot, sliced
1 tablespoon chives, finely chopped
1 tablespoon parsley, finely chopped

IN A MEDIUM-SIZED POT, bring stock to a simmer and add potatoes and celery root. Simmer until fork tender, about 6 to 7 minutes. Remove to a bowl and set aside.

HEAT OLIVE OIL IN A SMALL SKILLET over medium-high heat. When oil is shimmering, add shallot. Cook for 2 minutes to soften and then add to potatoes along with chives and parsley.

MASH TOGETHER with a potato masher. Taste for seasoning and stir in 1 teaspoon of olive oil.

POTATO CROQUETTES WITH
Caramelized Red Onions and Peas

2 tablespoons olive oil
½ red onion, sliced
3 sprigs fresh thyme (leaves only), finely chopped (or ½ teaspoon dried thyme)
1 teaspoon lemon zest
½ cup frozen peas, thawed for 10 minutes
1 tablespoon parsley, chopped
½ pound cooked potatoes (boiled, mashed, or roasted)
1 egg
¼ cup breadcrumbs (plain or panko)
½ cup sour cream blended with 1 tablespoon of *All Purpose Spice Blend* (page 29)
2 tablespoons chives, finely chopped

IN A MEDIUM-SIZED PAN, heat 1 tablespoon of oil over medium-high heat. When oil is shimmering, add onions, thyme, and lemon zest. Cook until onions soften without browning, about 5 minutes. Add peas, parsley, and stir to combine. Take off the heat and cover for 10 minutes to steam the peas. Transfer to a bowl.

ADD THE POTATOES, egg, and breadcrumbs to the onion and peas mixture. Mix thoroughly using your hands or a wooden spoon. Form the mixture into 4 balls, cover with plastic wrap, and refrigerate for 30 minutes.

RETURN PAN TO STOVETOP. Heat remaining 1 tablespoon of olive oil over a medium-high heat and when shimmering, gently place potato balls into the pan. Gently press down to form 1½-inch thick croquettes. Once brown and crispy, about 3 to 4 minutes, turn and cook the second side until brown. Remove to a plate lined with paper towel to absorb excess oil. Serve with smoky sour cream and chives.

As a kid, I always mixed my peas and mashed potatoes together, so this side dish brings back a lot of great home-cooked memories. The sweetness from the caramelized red onions and slight tanginess from the lemon zest take these croquettes to another level. This dish makes great use of leftover mashed or roasted potatoes.

Serves 4

Desserts are one of the easiest ways to use overripe fruit, day-old breads, and excess ingredients in your refrigerator and pantry. We typically buy more fruit than we actually eat and so much of it goes bad and gets thrown out. Overripe fruit can be a satisfying ingredient for a naturally sweet dessert.

CHAPTER 14: GRAND FINALES

Desserts from Light to Luscious

BANANA CROISSANT BREAD PUDDING
with Nutella

4 eggs
½ cup milk
1 teaspoon vanilla
½ teaspoon cinnamon
¼ teaspoon nutmeg
Pinch of salt
Vegetable spray
¼ cup granulated sugar
2 day-old croissants, torn into 1-inch pieces
2 very ripe bananas cut into ¼-inch slices
4 tablespoons Nutella, warmed in the microwave for 20 seconds

PREHEAT OVEN TO 350°F.

IN A MEDIUM-SIZED BOWL, whisk eggs, milk, vanilla, spices, and salt. Don't worry if the cinnamon clumps a bit. Set aside.

LIGHTLY SPRAY 2 (6-OUNCE) RAMEKINS with vegetable spray and sprinkle 1 teaspoon of the sugar in each. Roll around the sugar so that it sticks to the sprayed bottom of the ramekin.

PLACE ONE LAYER OF SLICED BANANAS in each ramekin, followed by half the croissant pieces. Sprinkle with 1 teaspoon of sugar, place another layer of banana, and drizzle 1 tablespoon of Nutella on top of each. Add the remaining croissant to the top of the ramekins.

SLOWLY POUR AN EQUAL AMOUNT OF EGG MIXTURE on top of the croissant. With your fingers, gently press the croissant into the egg mixture. Refrigerate for 20 minutes to set.

BEFORE PLACING IN THE OVEN, place a layer of overlapping banana slices over each ramekin and sprinkle remaining sugar on the top. Bake in the oven for 30 minutes. The bread pudding should puff substantially and spring back when you press it. Let cool for 5 minutes before serving. Garnish with a drizzle of Nutella.

For some reason, I over-buy croissants for the house and there are always two or three left the next day. This classic dessert uses day-old croissants, overripe bananas, and a few tablespoons of Nutella. You can substitute any several days-old bread to alter the flavor accordingly. Any overripe fruit will do, including strawberries, blueberries, peaches, or nectarines. If you don't have Nutella (and I don't know why you wouldn't), use any chocolate syrup available or add a handful of chocolate chips.

Serves 2

ROASTED PEARS WITH RUM MAPLE CREAM

2 pears, halved
2 cups water
½ cup light rum
3 tablespoons butter
¼ cup light brown sugar
¼ cup maple syrup
½ teaspoon cinnamon (plus extra for finishing)
¼ cup raisins
¼ cup dried cranberries
1 teaspoon vanilla
½ cup heavy cream

PREHEAT OVEN TO 350°F.

USING A TEASPOON OR PARING KNIFE, remove the core of each pear half. Leave the skin on. Place pear halves in a medium pot with water and rum. Bring to a boil and then take off heat and cover for 5 minutes while you make the sauce.

IN A NON-STICK PAN, melt the butter, then add the brown sugar, maple syrup, and cinnamon. Stir over a medium heat until mixture begins to bubble. Take pear halves out of the water and place them face down into the syrupy mixture. Add raisins and cranberries and place pan in the oven for 15 minutes. If pan has a plastic handle, wrap the handle with foil to prevent it from burning.

REMOVE THE PEARS FROM THE PAN and set them on platters, 2 halves for each serving.

RETURN PAN TO STOVETOP and over medium heat, add cream and vanilla. Bring mixture to a light simmer. Stir until sauce thickens, about 3 minutes. Spoon the sauce generously over the pears and sprinkle with cinnamon.

This dessert takes less than 20 minutes and is equally as delicious and decadent with peaches, nectarines, or apples.

DARK CHOCOLATE COCONUT
Macaroon Cookies

Are you ready for the perfect macaroon? Gotta give Mom credit for this one. My family has enjoyed these tasty chewy bits of coconut heaven for decades. Imagine my surprise when she finally told me she uses three ingredients and takes only twenty minutes. This is one of the simplest recipes on the planet . . . and one of the most delicious! The Epicure with Love version of this cookie is over ½ pound and packed with dark chocolate chunks. For a treat on the second day, warm macaroons in the oven or toaster oven to get them crispy.

Makes 15 to 20 macaroons

- 1 package (7-ounce) sweetened shredded coconut
- 1 egg, lightly beaten
- 3 tablespoon butter, melted
- ½ cup dark chocolate chips (optional)

PREHEAT OVEN TO 325°F.

COMBINE COCONUT, EGG, melted butter, and chocolate in a bowl and mix well. Using a spoon, drop tablespoon-size mounds on a parchment-lined cookie sheet and bake for 20 minutes or until lightly brown.

REMOVE IMMEDIATELY from the cookie sheet with a thin metal spatula. Place the macaroons on a wire rack and let cool for 1 hour before serving.

MIXED FRUIT CRISP

FILLING

3 apples, cored and cut into 1-inch chunks

2 pears, halved, cored, and cut into 1-inch chunks

1 peach, remove pit and cut into same size pieces as other fruit

1 cup mixed berries

1 lemon, zested and juiced

3 tablespoons flour

¼ cup granulated sugar

¼ cup light brown sugar

1 teaspoon cinnamon

½ teaspoon nutmeg

CRUMB TOPPING

1 cup flour

½ cup light brown sugar

¾ cup oatmeal, old-fashioned rolled oats

½ cup almonds (whole)

1 stick (4 ounces) butter, melted

½ teaspoon salt

PREHEAT OVEN TO 350°F.

FILLING

COMBINE ALL FILLING INGREDIENTS in a large bowl and mix well. Pour into a greased 13 by 9-inch glass baking dish.

CRUMB TOPPING

PLACE ALL TOPPING INGREDIENTS except butter, into a food processor and pulse 5 times to grind the almonds and combine thoroughly.

TOP THE FRUIT WITH CRUMB mixture and pour melted butter evenly over the top. Bake until fruit is bubbling on the sides, about 40 minutes. Place a sheet of foil or large baking sheet on the bottom rack of the oven to catch any fruit that bubbles over. Allow to cool for at least ten minutes before serving.

One of the favorite desserts my family and I enjoy is a warm fruit crisp. This is a fantastic way to use up overripe fruit. My sister, Deb, taught me a version that calls for pouring melted butter over the flour and sugar for a delicious crispy top. Feel free to use whatever fruit you have on hand such as nectarines, berries, or any variety of apples.

Serves 8

VANILLA BERRY CUSTARD

This simple delicious custard is a great way to use up that last handful of berries.

Serves 2

3 egg yolks
1 tablespoon granulated
   sugar
½ teaspoon vanilla
½ cup light cream
Handful of mixed berries
   (about ½ cup)
1 tablespoon brown sugar

PREHEAT OVEN TO 350°F.

SLOWLY HEAT THE CREAM in a small pot over a medium-low heat. When cream begins to show small bubbles on the edges, remove from heat.

IN A SMALL BOWL, blend the egg yolks, sugar, and vanilla. Pour about one third of the warm cream into the bowl to temper the eggs. Whisk with a fork to blend and pour egg mixture into the pot over a medium heat. Continuously whisk the mixture until it begins to thicken. Pour into ramekins, drop berries into the custard, and sprinkle the top with brown sugar.

BAKE FOR 12 TO 15 MINUTES until custard is mostly set. Remove from oven and let cool as the custard will continue to set. Refrigerate or serve room temperature.

STRAWBERRY CHEESECAKE BARS

CRUST
1 tablespoon sugar
⅛ teaspoon cinnamon
5 graham crackers
3 tablespoon butter, melted (plus 1 tablespoon for greasing baking dish)

FILLING
1 package (8-ounce) cream cheese
1 egg
1 lemon, zested and juiced
¼ cup granulated sugar
½ cup strawberries, tops cut off and sliced

PREHEAT OVEN TO 325°F.

CRUST

GREASE A 5 BY 9-INCH baking dish with butter or cooking spray. Cut a piece of parchment paper to fit in baking dish with 3 inches of excess hanging over two sides (approximately 11 by 9 inches).

IN A FOOD PROCESSOR, combine the sugar, cinnamon, and graham crackers until you have the texture of bread crumbs, not more than 10 seconds. Add the melted butter and pulse a couple of times to fully blend together. Pour the mixture into baking dish and gently pat down crumbs with the base of a glass. Bake in the oven until golden, about 12 minutes. Remove from oven and set aside to cool.

FILLING

ADD THE CREAM CHEESE, egg, lemon zest, lemon juice, and sugar to the food processor and pulse until well combined and smooth. Pour into baking dish and gently drop sliced strawberries into batter. They will sink slightly into the batter.

BAKE IN THE OVEN FOR 30 MINUTES, remove from the oven, and cool completely before refrigerating for at least 2 hours. Once set, lift out of baking dish by the parchment "handles" and using a sharp wet knife, cut in half lengthwise. Then cut crosswise into 1½-inch bars. Dust the top with confectioners' sugar.

What better way to use up cream cheese, graham crackers, and strawberries than a creamy, tangy, delicious homemade cheesecake? The hardest part is waiting the 2 hours for it to cool in the refrigerator. Sometimes I like to use muffin cups. If you want to double the recipe, bake in a 9 by 9-inch glass baking dish or 9-inch pie pan. You can use any sliced berries or leave them out altogether for a classic plain cheesecake.

Makes 10 bars

THE ULTIMATE CHOCOLATE
Chip Cookies

This cookie dough recipe can be adapted to incorporate many other ingredients in your pantry. Add ½ cup of peanut butter and a handful of mixed nuts or a large scoop of Nutella for the most amazing chewy, nutty cookie.

Makes 12 to 15 cookies

1 cup cake flour
⅔ cup bread flour or
   unbleached white flour
1 teaspoon baking powder
½ teaspoon baking soda
1 teaspoon salt
6 ounces butter
¾ cup light brown sugar
½ granulated sugar
2 eggs
1 tablespoon vanilla
8 ounces dark chocolate
   chips
4 ounces white chocolate
   chips

PREHEAT OVEN TO 350°F.

SIFT DRY INGREDIENTS INTO A BOWL. On a low speed, cream butter and sugar together using a mixer with a paddle attachment or hand mixer. Scrap the sides of the bowl and the paddle with a plastic spatula. On a high speed, add eggs one at a time. Lower speed to medium and add vanilla. Continue on medium speed and slowly add dry ingredients until blended. Scrap bottom of bowl and sides.

ADD CHOCOLATE CHIPS and blend for 5 seconds. (If using peanut butter or Nutella, add with the chips.) Place bowl in refrigerator for 30 minutes to firm up the dough.

USING A SCOOP and wet hands, portion the dough into 12 (4-ounce) balls. Place dough balls on a cookie sheet lined with parchment paper approximately 2 inches apart. Press down cookie dough balls slightly and bake for 15 to 18 minutes. Edges of cookies should begin to brown and the middle of cookies still slightly uncooked. Remove from oven and let cool for 10 minutes. Remove from cookie sheet and continue cooling on a baking rack.

STRAWBERRY AND CRANBERRY
Protein Bars

2 apples, cored, peeled, and cut into 2-inch chunks
½ cup vanilla soy milk
2 cups strawberry protein powder
1½ cups rolled oats
¼ cup flaxseed
¾ cup Grape Nuts cereal
½ cup egg whites
½ cup dried cranberries

PREHEAT OVEN TO 350°F. Grease 9 by 9-inch baking dish with vegetable spray. Cut a piece of parchment paper to fit in baking dish with 3 inches of excess hanging over two sides (approximately 15 by 9-inches).

PLACE APPLES AND SOY MILK in a small pot over medium heat. When milk begins to bubble, take off heat and let apples soften, about 10 minutes. Remove apples and place in a mini food processor and pulse 5 to 6 times to purée. Scoop out the purée and set aside to cool.

IN A LARGE BOWL, combine all the dry ingredients, apple purée, heated milk, egg whites, and dried cranberries. Mix well and pour into baking dish. Bake for 25 minutes, until a toothpick inserted into the middle comes out clean. Remove from the oven and immediately lift out using the parchment "handles." Cut into 10 rectangular bars while still warm.

Michele and I love protein bars and look for ones that are low in fat and carbs and high in protein. We decided to make our own and these utilize lots of existing pantry items as well as the last couple of apples on our kitchen counter.

Makes 10 bars

CHAPTER 15: THANKS FOR EVERYTHING

Holiday-Ever-After Dishes

Many households that cook for the holidays are left with more food than can fit in the refrigerator and freezer. The recipes in this chapter take the best of your holiday table and turn them into entirely new delicious dishes.

HOLIDAY HASH

This delicious hash makes use of just about everything from your holiday meal. I've incorporated turkey, ham, potatoes, stuffing, and vegetables into this crispy savory day-after dish. Use what you have. Add leftover mashed potatoes, sweet potatoes, cranberry sauce, even that last bit of gravy! Great as a side dish with a bowl of soup or serve as a main course with a fresh salad.

Serves 4 to 6

1 cup cooked turkey, torn
   into bite-size pieces (white
   or dark meat, or both)
1 cup cooked ham, torn into
   bite-size pieces (optional)
½ pound roasted potatoes or
   1 cup mashed potato
½ cup stuffing
½ cup cooked green beans,
   or mixed vegetables
¼ cup cranberry sauce
1 egg
1 tablespoon olive oil
¼ cup cheddar cheese,
   shredded (optional)

COMBINE ALL INGREDIENTS (except cheese) in a bowl and mix well.

IN A MEDIUM OR LARGE SKILLET, heat oil over a medium-high heat. When oil is shimmering, add hash mixture in one large ball. Press down with the back of a wooden spoon or spatula until the hash reaches the edge of the pan, forming a 2-inch thick pancake. Cook for 3 minutes until brown and flip to the other side. Continue cooking until second side is brown and crispy, about 3 minutes. Remove to a cutting board. While still warm, cut into wedges, sprinkle with cheese, and serve immediately. Also delicious served with applesauce, sour cream, warmed gravy, or cranberry sauce.

GREEN BEAN AND TURKEY MEATBALLS

These meatballs are terrific accompanied by a serving of rice with a squeeze of lemon or with pasta and olive oil. I eat them with a heaping spoonful of cranberry sauce.

Makes 6

2 tablespoons olive oil
½ onion, chopped
2 garlic cloves, minced
1 cup cooked turkey, torn into bite-size pieces
½ cup cooked green beans (or string beans)
1 egg
¼ cup breadcrumbs
¼ cup Parmesan cheese, grated
1 tablespoon parsley, finely chopped
Salt
1 lemon
Cranberry sauce (optional)

IN A SMALL SKILLET heat 1 tablespoon of oil over a medium-high heat. When oil is shimmering, add onions and garlic. Cook until vegetables are soft but not brown, about 5 minutes. Remove from heat to cool.

IN A MEDIUM BOWL, combine remaining ingredients and cooled onions. Taste for seasoning. With wet hands, form a medium-sized meatball. If mixture seems too dry and doesn't hold together, add a tablespoon of milk or water to bind. If mixture is too wet, add a tablespoon or two of breadcrumbs. When mixture is just right, form into balls and refrigerate for 20 minutes to set.

WIPE OUT THE SKILLET with a sheet of paper towel and heat 1 tablespoon of oil over a medium-high heat. When oil is shimmering, add meatballs. Carefully turn meatballs to brown on all sides, about 3 to 4 minutes. Cook in batches if pan is too crowded. Place cooked meatballs on a paper towel–lined plate or platter to absorb excess oil. Serve with a squeeze of lemon and a spoonful of cranberry sauce.

TURKEY AND RICE

This dish is holiday-after comfort food at its best. You can use leftover rice and can substitute chicken or ham for the turkey. Serve with a squeeze of lemon or, for an Asian twist, sprinkle soy sauce and sesame seeds over the finished dish.

Serves 4
1 tablespoon olive oil
½ onion, finely chopped
1 garlic clove, minced
¾ cup long grain rice or 2 cups cooked rice
1½ cups stock (vegetable, chicken, turkey) or water
1 sprig fresh rosemary, plus 1 sprig for garnish
1 cup cooked turkey, torn into bite-size pieces
½ cup cooked carrots and green beans or cooked mixed vegetables

IN A MEDIUM-SIZED POT, heat oil over a medium-high heat. When oil is shimmering, add onions and garlic. Cook until soft but not brown, about 5 minutes. Add rosemary and rice. Stir to coat the rice, about 1 minute. Add stock, a pinch of salt, and give the rice a gentle stir. Cover and cook until all the liquid is absorbed, about 20 minutes.

WITH 5 MINUTES LEFT, stir in turkey and vegetables so they get warmed through as the rice finishes cooking. Serve immediately with a squeeze of lemon. Garnish with fresh rosemary leaves.

ROASTED BUTTERNUT SQUASH AND PUMPKIN SOUP

This soup has become one of the biggest sellers of the Epicure with Love soups. It's smooth and comforting and is reminiscent of last night's pumpkin pie. The twist here is the curry powder, which gives the soup an unexpected yet subtle kick.

Serves 6

2 tablespoons butter
2 leeks, cleaned and sliced into ½-inch rings (see page 99 for *How To Clean Leeks*)
3 quarts stock (vegetable, chicken, turkey)
2 butternut squash (approximately 4 pounds), peeled, halved and deseeded (cut into 1-inch cubes)
1 potato, peeled and diced
1 cup milk
½ cup pumpkin purée
3 tablespoons light brown sugar
2 teaspoons curry powder
1 teaspoon cinnamon
½ teaspoon salt
½ teaspoon nutmeg

IN A STOCK POT, melt the butter over a medium-high heat. Add leeks and cook until softened but not brown, about 3 minutes. Remove 2 tablespoons of the cooked leeks for garnish. Add stock and squash and simmer for 5 minutes. Add potatoes and continue simmering until potatoes and squash are fork tender, about 10 minutes.

IN A BOWL, whisk together the milk, pumpkin purée, sugar, and spices. Set aside.

USING AN IMMERSION BLENDER, purée the soup until smooth.

(You can use a traditional blender or food processor by puréeing in batches. Return puréed soup to pot.)

ADD PUMPKIN AND SPICES MIXTURE to soup pot and continue simmering for additional 5 minutes. Taste for seasoning. Serve with cooked leeks.

IF USING LEFTOVER COOKED SQUASH . . . add after potatoes are cooked. Allow squash to warm through, then purée.

SWEET POTATO AND HAM CROQUETTES

I have always loved the combination of sweet potatoes and ham. My good friend Tom insists he created the ham and mashed sweet potato sandwich, which he says he eagerly looks forward to the day after Thanksgiving. Regular mashed or roasted potatoes will work just as well but may need a bit of help from some fresh herbs such as thyme, parsley, basil, chervil, or rosemary. You can also kick up this recipe with some crumbled bacon.

Serves 2

2 tablespoons olive oil
1 shallot, sliced
1 cup cooked sweet potato (mashed)
½ cup cooked ham, torn into bite-size pieces
1 tablespoon parsley, finely chopped
½ cup breadcrumbs
1 tablespoon *BBQ Spice Blend* (page 34)

IN A NON-STICK SKILLET, heat 1 tablespoon of oil over a medium heat. When oil is shimmering, add shallot and cook until softened, about 3 minutes.

COMBINE SWEET POTATO, ham, parsley, ¼ cup of the breadcrumbs and cooled shallot in a medium-sized bowl. With wet hands, form 4 equal balls and place in the refrigerator for 30 minutes to set.

COMBINE REMAINING BREADCRUMBS and spice blend in a shallow dish or plate. Press each potato and ham ball into the breadcrumbs, forming a 1½-inch thick patty. Gently turn the patty to adhere breadcrumbs to second side.

WIPE OUT THE PAN with a sheet of paper towel and add 1 tablespoon of oil over a medium-high heat. When oil is shimmering, add the breaded croquettes and brown on both sides, about 5 minutes total. Serve immediately.

PECAN PIE COOKIES

This cookie utilizes my Ultimate Chocolate Chip Cookie Dough with the addition of leftover pecan pie. Sounds funny, but pecan pie lovers are going to be very happy. You can leave out the chocolate chips and add a slice of pumpkin or sweet potato pie for a sweet cookie that is filled with holiday spice.

2 pounds *The Ultimate Chocolate Chip Cookie* dough (page 256),
  chocolate chips optional
1 slice pecan pie

PREHEAT OVEN TO 350°F.

PLACE PECAN PIE SLICE in a mini food processor and pulse 5 times. Scrape out the pie bits with a plastic spatula and add to softened cookie dough. Mix thoroughly and refrigerate for 30 minutes.

USING A SCOOP and wet hands, portion the dough into 12 (4-ounce) balls. Place dough balls on a cookie sheet lined with parchment paper approximately 2 inches apart. Press down cookie dough balls slightly and bake for 15 to 18 minutes. Edges of the cookies should begin to brown and the middle of cookies still slightly uncooked.

REMOVE FROM OVEN and let cool for 10 minutes. Remove from cookie sheet and continue cooling on a baking rack.

CRANBERRY MAPLE WALNUT MUFFINS

Cooking spray
1 cup cake flour
1 teaspoon baking powder
1 teaspoon baking soda
½ teaspoon salt
½ cup light brown sugar
1 egg
4 tablespoons butter, melted
½ cup milk
½ teaspoon maple extract
   (or 1 tablespoon maple
   syrup)
½ cup cranberry sauce
½ cup chopped walnuts
2 tablespoons rolled oats

PREHEAT OVEN TO 350°F.
Grease muffin tins with cooking spray or drop in paper muffin cups.

SIFT FLOUR, baking powder, baking soda, and salt into a large mixing bowl. In a separate bowl, whisk together sugar, egg, butter, milk, and maple extract until smooth.

ADD WET MIXTURE TO DRY INGREDIENTS and with a wooden spoon, gently mix until mostly combined. Leave a few dry spots throughout the batter. Fold in the cranberry sauce and walnuts and pour into muffin tins. Leave ½-inch space from the top. Sprinkle the tops with the oats and bake until golden and the muffins have risen above the tins, about 15 minutes.

REMOVE FROM OVEN and let cool, about 15 minutes. Remove from the muffin tin and place on a wire rack to continue cooling, another 15 minutes.

Muffins are a great way to use up overripe fruit, nuts, and even savory ingredients such as cooked vegetables and cheese.

Makes 10 to 12 muffins

"STUFFLE"

Find your waffle iron and bring out the stuffing for an incredibly delicious treat and a great way to get your family involved in making breakfast on the day after Thanksgiving. This waffle is as good as your stuffing. For a touch of sweetness, add dried cranberries or diced apples to your stuffing before making the "stuffle." I love it with lots of maple syrup.

Serves 4

6 cups stuffing
2 eggs
Cooking spray
Maple syrup or cranberry
   sauce

HEAT YOUR WAFFLE IRON according to its directions.

ADD EGGS TO STUFFING and mix until combined. Spray both sides of the waffle iron with cooking spray. Place 1½ cups of stuffing in the center of the waffle iron and close. Cook until brown and crispy (like a waffle). To keep cooked waffles warm, place in the oven directly on the rack at 250°F until all your waffles are ready. Serve with maple syrup or cranberry sauce.

CHAPTER 16: CHEERS

Cocktails Worth "Salvaging" For

I love the fact that herbs have made their way into so many contemporary cocktails. These drink recipes are a great way to use up wilted herbs, citrus fruits, and juices.

GRAPEFRUIT POMEGRANATE MARTINI

Serves 2

4 ounces vodka
3 ounces pomegranate juice
6 ounces fresh grapefruit juice
1 ounce strawberry liqueur
lime wedges

ADD ICE ⅔ OF THE WAY in a shaker and add all ingredients except lime wedges. Shake vigorously and strain into chilled martini glasses. Squeeze lime wedge into each glass and drop into the martini. Serve immediately.

SWEET BASIL GIN MARTINI

Serves 2

BASIL SIMPLE SYRUP
1 cup granulated sugar
1 cup water
1 lemon, rind peeled into 3
   strips (¼-inch each)
4 to 5 basil leaves

MARTINIS
6 ounces gin
3 ounces melon liqueur
2 tablespoons basil simple
   syrup
basil leaves for garnish

BASIL SIMPLE SYRUP

Combine water, sugar, lemon strips, and basil in a medium pot. Stir and bring to a boil. Cover and take off heat for 20 minutes and then allow to cool. Strain and set aside.

MARTINIS

For 2 martinis, add ice ⅔ of the way in a shaker cup. Add gin, melon liqueur, and basil simple syrup. Shake vigorously. Strain into sugar-rimmed martini glasses and garnish with basil leaf.

RIMMING THE GLASSES

Dip the rim of each martini glass into the cooled basil simple syrup and then onto a plate with some granulated sugar. Tap the glass gently to shake off excess sugar.

PEPPER VODKA BLOODY MARY

Serves 4

1 quart tomato or vegetable juice
3 tablespoons celery salt
2 tablespoons Worcestershire sauce
2 tablespoons white horseradish
1 teaspoon chili paste
2 limes, quartered
8 ounces pepper vodka
1 tablespoon smoked paprika (for glass rims)
Green olives (garnish)
Celery stalks (garnish)

CHILL 4 BEER MUGS IN THE FREEZER. In a large pitcher, combine juice, two tablespoons of celery salt, Worcestershire, horseradish, and chili paste. Squeeze all the lime quarters into pitcher except one, which you will use to rim the glasses. Stir well and refrigerate for an hour.

ON A SMALL PLATE, blend 1 tablespoon each of paprika and celery salt with a fork. Rim the chilled beer mugs with lime and then invert each mug onto the plate. Fill each mug with ice and then add 2 ounces of vodka. Pour the juice mixture to the top and stir. Garnish with large green olives and a large stalk of celery.

GREEN MELON AND CUCUMBER MARTINI

Serves 2

CUCUMBER SIMPLE SYRUP

1 cup granulated sugar
1 cup water
½ cucumber, cut into ¼-inch slices (other ½ for martini)
½ cup honeydew melon, cut into chunks (plus ¼ cup for garnish)
Handful of cilantro

MARTINI

½ cucumber, peeled, seeded and diced
1 lime, quartered
2 tablespoons cucumber/ melon simple syrup
4 ounces vodka
2 ounces melon liqueur
½ ounce Rose;s Lime Juice

CUCUMBER SIMPLE SYRUP

COMBINE WATER, SUGAR, cucumber slices, melon chunks, and cilantro in a medium pot. Stir and bring to a boil. Cover and take off heat for 20 minutes and then uncover and allow to cool. Strain and set aside.

MARTINIS

For 2 martinis, add ½ cup of diced cucumber to a large shaker along with 1 lime quarter and cucumber simple syrup. Using the back of a spoon, muddle the ingredients into a chunky pulp. Add ice, vodka, melon liqueur, and lime juice and place the lid securely on top of the shaker. Shake vigorously. Strain into martini glasses.

IF YOU LIKE YOUR COCKTAIL a bit sweeter, pour a little simple syrup on the top of each drink. If you like more tartness, squeeze a fresh lime quarter into the martini just before serving. Garnish with cilantro and melon chunk.

CITRUS & ELDERFLOWER SCREWDRIVER MARTINI

Serves 4

8 ounces vodka
2 ounces Elderflower liqueur
2 oranges, juiced
1 lemon, juiced
1 grapefruit, juiced
2 tablespoons granulated sugar (for rimming the glasses)
Orange zest for garnish

COMBINE VODKA, LIQUEUR, and fresh juices in a large pitcher. Refrigerate for 1 hour. While the mixture is chilling, fill a small plate with extra lemon juice and another with granulated sugar. Dip the rims of the glasses into the lemon juice and then gently onto the sugar. Chill the glasses in the refrigerator until ready to serve.

TO SERVE, FILL SHAKER ⅔ OF THE WAY with ice and pour mixture from the pitcher until liquid reaches the top of the ice. Shake vigorously for 10 seconds and strain into the chilled sugar-rimmed glasses. Sprinkle a little orange zest on the surface and serve immediately.

GINGER-INFUSED STRAWBERRY MANGO BELLINI

Serves 4

GINGER SIMPLE SYRUP
1 cup granulated sugar
1 cup water
½-inch piece ginger root,
    cut into six slices

BELLINIS
½ cup frozen mango
½ cup frozen strawberries
1 bottle Champagne
Chill 4 champagne flutes in the freezer.

GINGER SIMPLE SYRUP: In a small pot, bring sugar, water, and ginger root to a boil. Once liquid begins to boil, take it off the heat and cover. Let stand for 20 minutes to cool. Strain and set aside.

BELLINIS: In a blender, purée the fruit with all the ginger simple syrup. When ready to serve, fill champagne glass ⅓ of the way up with purée. Slowly pour chilled champagne to the top.

JACK 'N' CHILL—JACK DANIELS & FROZEN LIMEADE

My friends Cindy and Michael inspired this drink. We wanted a refreshing cocktail but didn't have a mixer or juice. Cindy pulled out the frozen limeade, Michael grabbed a bottle of whiskey, and the rest is history!

Serves 4

8 ounces whiskey or
  bourbon
1 can of frozen limeade,
  slightly thawed
1 lime, cut into wedges

CHILL 4 (8-OUNCE) ROCKS GLASSES in the freezer.

IN A BLENDER, combine whiskey and limeade. If limeade is partially frozen then you don't need to add ice. If limeade is completely thawed, add 1 cup of ice to the blender. Blend until smooth.

POUR INTO CHILLED GLASSES. Squeeze a couple of lime wedges on top of each of the frozen drinks and drop in.

LEMON LIME WHISKEY

Serves 4

8 ounces whiskey
8 ounces freshly squeezed lemon juice
8 ounces freshly squeezed lime juice
8 ounces club soda (or sparkling water)
Lemon and lime slices for garnish

FILL 4 (8-OUNCE) ROCKS GLASSES with ice. Pour 2 ounces of whiskey in each and swirl to coat the ice. Pour 2 ounces each of lemon and lime juice in each glass followed by 2 ounces of club soda. Stir with a spoon and garnish with 1 lemon slice and 1 lime slice.

MINT HOT CHOCOLATE
for Grown-ups

Serves 4

20 ounces milk
¼ cup granulated sugar
8 ounces semi-sweet chocolate (chips)
2 teaspoons ground cinnamon
2 teaspoons vanilla extract
4 ounces peppermint schnapps (or crème de menthe)
1 cup heavy cream, whipped until thick and forms peaks
4 ounces white chocolate, shavings (block or bar)

POUR MILK INTO MEDIUM-SIZED POT and heat over a low heat. Whisk in the sugar until mostly dissolved. Do not let the milk simmer. Remove from heat, add chips, cinnamon, and vanilla extract and continue whisking until chocolate is completely melted and mixture is completely blended.

POUR 1 OUNCE of schnapps into the bottom of each coffee mug. Carefully pour milk mixture into each mug, leaving 1-inch of space at the top.

TOP WITH BIG DOLLOP (2 TABLESPOONS) of whipped cream and sprinkle with white chocolate shavings and cinnamon. Serve immediately.

ABOUT EPICURE GOURMET MARKET & CAFÉ

Epicure Gourmet Market & Café began in 1945 as a small butcher shop owned by the Thal brothers. It grew as the city of Miami Beach prospered in the decades that followed, and the contents of the market expanded to include signature bakery products and prepared foods as well as the finest quality of ingredients, selected by professionals, each knowledgeable in their area of expertise.

In 1998, Epicure Market was purchased by the Starkman family from Los Angeles; the Starkmans were already involved in the food business as the owners of ten Jerry's Famous Deli locations in California. Epicure now has three locations. The one in Sunny Isles Beach opened in 2008 and contains a full-service restaurant and bar along with a more casual café, while the original store, recently renovated, remains in South Beach. A third location in historic Coral Gables opened in fall 2013 and features more than 25,000 square feet of retail space plus outdoor seating for their full-service restaurant and café. Several more Epicure locations are being planned, including two more in South Florida and an expansion of the successful retail/restaurant concept on the West Coast.

In 2009, Epicure Gourmet Market became the home for Chef Michael Love's series of cooking classes, titled Cooking with Love. Jason Starkman and Michael Love collaborated on a cobranded food line, Epicure with Love, which launched in 2011. The freshly made food contains no preservatives and runs the gamut from 8 Vegetable Purée Soup and Vegetarian Wild Mushroom Bisque to Bacon, Onion, & Truffle Four Cheese Mac 'n' Cheese, Spiced Pumpkin Cornbread, a line of eight-inch Chunk Cookies, and four different brownies. Epicure with Love now includes ten all-natural soups and twelve bakery items. Many of the Epicure with Love recipes are in the *Salvage Chef Cookbook*.

ACKNOWLEDGMENTS

This book has been a collaboration of so many people and I am grateful for the support and assistance that my family, friends, and coworkers have given me. It has taken more than four years to complete and would not have happened at all if it weren't for my friendship and partnership with Jason Starkman.

Huge thanks to Lynn Parks for not only her exceptional talent as my food photographer and food stylist, but for being a fan of my food and believing in me and this project from day one. Thanks to Ellen Brown for your tough love and book expertise, which put me on the proper path to getting published. A big thank-you to Kim Weiss for her advice and support, which helped me focus on the things that make for a successful book.

To all the employees and managers at Epicure Gourmet Market & Café who supported the launch of the Epicure with Love product line and have allowed me to become a permanent part of the Epicure family. Special thanks to my peeps in the meat department, including Cesar, Harvey, Monica, George, Juan, Miguel, Taz, and especially Rudi, who has given me not only his friendship, amazing ideas, and recipes, but who also took the time to share his ridiculously vast wealth of knowledge with me. I'd like to also thank Epicure's general managers Mark, Diane, Oscar, and Harold, who created the supportive environment for me to grow as a chef.

I am exceedingly grateful to my incredible agent, business manager, and friend Alan Morell of Creative Management Partners, who not only makes everything happen, but also continuously believes in me and never ceases to amaze me with what he brings to the table. Super thanks to my literary coagent Regina Brooks and the Serendipity Literary Agency for bringing me to Skyhorse Publishing. Thanks to Nicole Frail, my editor at Skyhorse, for her enthusiasm for my "salvage" concept and all her hard work on this project.

A huge thank-you to my executive producers Tim Troke (*Chefs Run Wild, The Salvage Chef*) and Mike Morris (*Diners, Drive-ins and Dives*). Tim has been a brilliant collaborator and mentor and continues to amaze me with his expertise, support, and most of all his friendship. Mike has inspired me and mentored me to be the best I can be in front of the camera and is a true professional in all ways. A sincere and warm thank you to my publicist, social media facilitator, and trusted friend Jacquelynn Powers. Her love of cooking, passion for cookbooks, over twenty years in the publishing business, and most of all her enthusiasm and friendship have made her an amazing addition to my team.

A giant thank-you and hug to my mother for . . . well, just about everything! From inspiration to never-ending support to daily (and nightly) editing, for ideas, and for keeping me from using too many adjectives in one sentence. Thanks to my sister, Deb, and my niece (and chef) Casey for editing my very first draft.

Thank you to my son, Miles, for being an amazing child who has displayed the understanding and compassion of an extremely mature person as I immersed myself in cooking and writing for the past four years.

Lastly, I'd like to thank the love of my life, Michele. Michele inspired me to go forward and turn a rough draft into a book, inspired many of the recipes in this book, was an amazing food stylist for the photo shoots, and had to make many sacrifices for me to make my deadlines.

SALVAGE INDEX

METRIC AND IMPERIAL CONVERSIONS

(These conversions are rounded for convenience)

Ingredient	Cups/Tablespoons/ Teaspoons	Ounces	Grams/Milliliters
Butter	1 cup=16 tablespoons= 2 sticks	8 ounces	230 grams
Cream cheese	1 tablespoon	0.5 ounce	14.5 grams
Cheese, shredded	1 cup	4 ounces	110 grams
Cornstarch	1 tablespoon	0.3 ounce	8 grams
Flour, all-purpose	1 cup/1 tablespoon	4.5 ounces/0.3 ounce	125 grams/8 grams
Flour, whole wheat	1 cup	4 ounces	120 grams
Fruit, dried	1 cup	4 ounces	120 grams
Fruits or veggies, chopped	1 cup	5 to 7 ounces	145 to 200 grams
Fruits or veggies, puréed	1 cup	8.5 ounces	245 grams
Honey, maple syrup, or corn syrup	1 tablespoon	.75 ounce	20 grams
Liquids: cream, milk, water, or juice	1 cup	8 fluid ounces	240 milliliters
Oats	1 cup	5.5 ounces	150 grams
Salt	1 teaspoon	0.2 ounces	6 grams
Spices: cinnamon, cloves, ginger, or nutmeg (ground)	1 teaspoon	0.2 ounce	5 milliliters
Sugar, brown, firmly packed	1 cup	7 ounces	200 grams
Sugar, white	1 cup/1 tablespoon	7 ounces/0.5 ounce	200 grams/12.5 grams
Vanilla extract	1 teaspoon	0.2 ounce	4 grams

OVEN TEMPERATURES

Fahrenheit	Celcius	Gas Mark
225°	110°	¼
250°	120°	½
275°	140°	1
300°	150°	2
325°	160°	3
350°	180°	4
375°	190°	5
400°	200°	6
425°	220°	7
450°	230°	8

NOTES

NOTES

NOTES

NOTES

NOTES

NOTES

NOTES